Food

Other Books of Related Interest:

At Issue Series
Ethanol
How Should Obesity Be Treated?

Current Controversies Series
Conserving the Environment
Fair Trade
The Global Food Crisis
The U.S. Economy
The World Economy

Global Viewpoints Series
Climate Change
Famine
Population Growth

Introducing Issues with Opposing Viewpoints Series
Globalization
Organic Food and Farming

Issues That Concern You
Dieting
Obesity
Vegetarianism

Opposing Viewpoints Series
Agricultural Subsidies
Health

GLOBALVIEWPOINTS

Food

Christina Fisanick, Book Editor

GREENHAVEN PRESS
A part of Gale, Cengage Learning

GALE
CENGAGE Learning™

Detroit • New York • San Francisco • New Haven, Conn • Waterville, Maine • London

Christine Nasso, *Publisher*
Elizabeth Des Chenes, *Managing Editor*

© 2010 Greenhaven Press, a part of Gale, Cengage Learning

Gale and Greenhaven Press are registered trademarks used herein under license.

For more information, contact:
Greenhaven Press
27500 Drake Rd.
Farmington Hills, MI 48331-3535
Or you can visit our Internet site at gale.cengage.com

For product information and technology assistance, contact us at

Gale Customer Support, 1-800-877-4253
For permission to use material from this text or product, submit all requests online at www.cengage.com/permissions

Further permissions questions can be emailed to permissionrequest@cengage.com

Articles in Greenhaven Press anthologies are often edited for length to meet page requirements. In addition, original titles of these works are changed to clearly present the main thesis and to explicitly indicate the author's opinion. Every effort is made to ensure that Greenhaven Press accurately reflects the original intent of the authors. Every effort has been made to trace the owners of copyrighted material.

Cover image © TWPhoto/Corbis.

LIBRARY OF CONGRESS CATALOGING-IN-PUBLICATION DATA

Food / Christina Fisanick, book editor.
    p. cm. -- (Global viewpoints)
    Includes bibliographical references and index.
    ISBN 978-0-7377-4723-2 (hardcover) -- ISBN 978-0-7377-4724-9 (pbk.)
    1. Food supply. 2. Food--Safety measures. 3. Food security. I. Fisanick, Christina.
    II. Series: Global viewpoints.
    HD9000.5.F547 2010
    363.8--dc22
                                                                2010010339

Printed in the United States of America
1 2 3 4 5 6 7 14 13 12 11 10

Contents

Chapter 2: Food Scarcity and Security

Chapter 3: Human Health and Food Safety

Regularly consuming meat is not healthy for humans. In addition, eating meat contributes to the world food shortage because of environmental pollutions generated from the raising of livestock and the preparation of meat for sale.

Foreword

"The problems of all of humanity can only be solved by all of humanity."
—Swiss author Friedrich Dürrenmatt

Global interdependence has become an undeniable reality. Mass media and technology have increased worldwide access to information and created a society of global citizens. Understanding and navigating this global community is a challenge, requiring a high degree of information literacy and a new level of learning sophistication.

Building on the success of its flagship series, *Opposing Viewpoints*, Greenhaven Press has created the *Global Viewpoints* series to examine a broad range of current, often controversial topics of worldwide importance from a variety of international perspectives. Providing students and other readers with the information they need to explore global connections and think critically about worldwide implications, each *Global Viewpoints* volume offers a panoramic view of a topic of widespread significance.

Drugs, famine, immigration—a broad, international treatment is essential to do justice to social, environmental, health, and political issues such as these. Junior high, high school, and early college students, as well as general readers, can all use *Global Viewpoints* anthologies to discern the complexities relating to each issue. Readers will be able to examine unique national perspectives while, at the same time, appreciating the interconnectedness that global priorities bring to all nations and cultures.

Material in each volume is selected from a diverse range of sources, including journals, magazines, newspapers, nonfiction books, speeches, government documents, pamphlets, organization newsletters, and position papers. *Global Viewpoints* is truly global, with material drawn primarily from international sources available in English and secondarily from U.S. sources with extensive international coverage.

Features of each volume in the *Global Viewpoints* series include:

- An **annotated table of contents** that provides a brief summary of each essay in the volume, including the name of the country or area covered in the essay.

- An **introduction** specific to the volume topic.

- A **world map** to help readers locate the countries or areas covered in the essays.

- For each viewpoint, an **introduction** that contains notes about the author and source of the viewpoint explains why material from the specific country is being presented, summarizes the main points of the viewpoint, and offers three **guided reading questions** to aid in understanding and comprehension.

- **For further discussion** questions that promote critical thinking by asking the reader to compare and contrast aspects of the viewpoints or draw conclusions about perspectives and arguments.

- A worldwide list of **organizations to contact** for readers seeking additional information.

- A **periodical bibliography** for each chapter and a **bibliography of books** on the volume topic to aid in further research.

- A comprehensive **subject index** to offer access to people, places, events, and subjects cited in the text, with the countries covered in the viewpoints highlighted.

Global Viewpoints is designed for a broad spectrum of readers who want to learn more about current events, history, political science, government, international relations, economics, environmental science, world cultures, and sociology— students doing research for class assignments or debates, teachers and faculty seeking to supplement course materials, and others wanting to understand current issues better. By presenting how people in various countries perceive the root causes, current consequences, and proposed solutions to worldwide challenges, *Global Viewpoints* volumes offer readers opportunities to enhance their global awareness and their knowledge of cultures worldwide.

Introduction

"The food crisis is not over in poor countries; addressing food security will require raising farmers' productivity and incomes."

> David Theis,
> World Bank,
> September 16, 2009

Ensuring enough food for everyone is one of the top priorities of most societies. Food scarcity creates social unrest and lowers productivity. Unfortunately, overfishing, overharvesting, pollution, and an ever-growing population have led to food shortages in nearly all parts of the globe. In addition, rising food costs, soaring oil prices, and a struggling global economy keep available food out of the hands of those people who need it. Although international aid organizations and governments are working toward a better distribution of resources, the challenges are formidable. A historical understanding of the relationship between humans and the food they need to survive can yield insight into this often complex situation.

At the dawn of human civilization, humans relied on hunting wild animals and gathering vegetables and other edible plants to sustain life. The so-called hunter-gatherers were nomadic, roving from one fertile location to another as they depleted resources. Although not the most efficient method of survival, Stone Age man managed to live off the land for millions of years. Not surprisingly, this sometimes precarious existence led to a diminished life span. According to the anthropologists at the National Museum of Denmark in Copenhagen, the average life span of humans during this period was only thirty-five years and infant mortality rates were high.

All that changed around ten thousand years ago when Neolithic man learned how to cultivate crops. Historians, such as Bamber Gascoigne of Historyworld.net, refer to these activities as "the most significant single development in human history." Remarkably, this revolution in the way humans survive occurred simultaneously in several parts of the globe. It is thought that the change in global temperatures after the Ice Age encouraged humans to stay in warm regions where plants were plentiful rather than take a chance on food scarcity in other areas. To encourage animals (an important part of the early human diet) to stay nearby, Neolithic man began growing crops. Within a few thousand years, the community of Jericho was founded near Jerusalem, and protective walls were built to keep other tribes out of the first city and agricultural center.

As humans domesticated animals and improved their agricultural skills, population and life expectancy rates grew, which allowed for the development of new tools and food preservation methods. However, these improvements were largely limited to temperate climates, mostly in the Middle East and Africa. In fact, hunting and gathering remained a way of life for many of the earth's people until the early twentieth century.

Advances in civilization, such as better tools and more knowledge about chemistry and biology, led to even further improvements in food security across the globe. Thriving cultures, including those in Europe and parts of the Americas, did so mostly because they were able to provide food for their people year-round, even in not-so-ideal climates. Preservation methods, especially those including salt as a drying agent, led to the flourishing of human culture and longer life spans. As archaeologist David Bloch notes in his online archives, "The power to control a population's salt supply was power over life and death."

The invention of affordable home cooling methods in conjunction with electricity further increased the capacity for stockpiling food, which made it possible for societies to prosper. In *Heat and Cold: Mastering the Great Indoors*, Ben Nagengast writes, "The household refrigerator changed the way people ate and socially affected the household." Meat, butter, milk, and other perishable foods could now be kept longer, and reliable refrigeration, as opposed to ice in iceboxes, reduced the likelihood of illnesses from spoiled food. In the February–March 2003 issue of *History Magazine*, Barbara Krasner-Khait notes that "by 1950, more than 80 percent of American farms and more than 90 percent of urban homes had one," referring to refrigerators. These rates were comparable in other industrialized nations of the time as well.

Unfortunately, not all inventions have led to improvements in the human condition. As many parts of the globe went through industrial growth, more people moved away from rural settings where they grew their own food and killed their own meat to urban centers where food was bought from others. Food quality could not be ensured, and foodborne illnesses actually increased. American writer Upton Sinclair revealed some of these dangers in *The Jungle*, his scathing attack of the meatpacking industry at the turn of the twentieth century. He revealed that the meat sold to the public was often diseased, contaminated, and rotten.

More recently, people in so-called first world, or industrialized, countries have faced another crisis that some experts say might be related to the growing distance between food producers and consumers: obesity. Dr. Boyd Swinburn, director of the World Health Organization's Collaborating Centre for Obesity Prevention, points to the rise in the availability of calorically dense, nutritionally empty foods as the biggest factor in expanding waistlines around the world. The dangers of obesity include heart disease, diabetes, and other severe diseases. Swinburn and his colleagues found that exercise, or lack thereof, was not a significant factor in weight gain, which seems contrary to previous reports.

However, other researchers have come forward to corroborate Swinburn's findings. In a 2006 issue of *Nature Clinical Practice Endocrinology & Metabolism*, pediatric endocrinologist Dr. Robert Lustig, argues that processed foods can have a toxic effect, especially on growing bodies. By their biochemical structure, processed foods encourage overconsumption and discourage exercise by inducing fatigue. Lustig concludes, "Although common wisdom dictates that obesity is an interaction between genetics and environment, the gene pool has not changed in the last thirty years, but the environment has." In other words, human physiology has not changed during this period of time, but food and the way it is consumed has changed.

Nonetheless, not everyone is convinced that access to a plentiful supply of affordable food is entirely negative. In fact, Daniel Ben-Ami writes in a September 9, 2005, article for Spiked-Online.com that the current obesity epidemic in wealthy countries, specifically in the United States, is merely a casualty of success. Ben-Ami argues, "to have achieved a situation where, at least in the developed world, food scarcity is virtually eliminated is a tremendous achievement." Although he thinks that obesity could lead to health complications and that food quality could be improved, "these are relatively small challenges compared with the historic battle to rid the world of the scourge of hunger."

As parts of the world continue to fight the great war against hunger, still others struggle with the sometimes deadly side effects of excess food. The authors in *Global Viewpoints: Food* debate current views on food in the following chapters: Food Safety and Regulation, Food Scarcity and Security, Human Health and Food Safety, and Food and the World Economy. These viewpoints reveal the constant debate about how to accomplish the one goal humans have struggled for throughout history: survival.

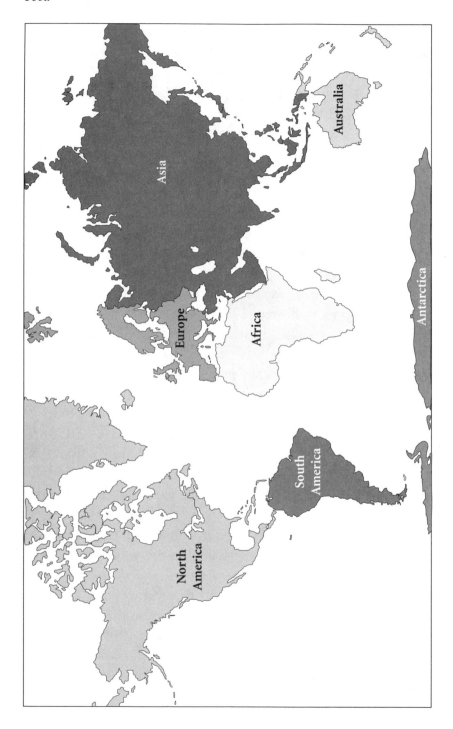

GLOBALVIEWPOINTS

CHAPTER 1

Food Safety and Regulation

International Food Safety Standards Are Needed

Oliver Cann

Oliver Cann is a regular contributor to Business Standards *and its online content. In the following viewpoint, Cann argues that the international food industry has been working toward global food standards, but there is much more work that needs to be done. He insists that the passage of new specifications for the growing, preparing, and shipping of food is the best possible scenario for an industry that is responsible for feeding the world.*

As you read, consider the following questions:

1. As of April 2009, how many food products were recalled?
2. About how long does it take a piece of fruit grown in Africa to reach store shelves in Europe?
3. How many world supermarket chains have committed to global food industry standards?

Early in 2009, the Food and Drug Administration (FDA) in the US [United States] announced that it had found widespread salmonella contamination at a large peanut processing plant based in Georgia. Despite the fact that the plant itself was not a major player, its products—in particular, its peanut paste—tainted an entire supply chain.

According to the FDA, as of April 2009, more than 2,100 products in 17 categories had been recalled by more than 200 companies, and the list continues to grow. The plant at the heart of the incident has filed for bankruptcy and the salmonella outbreak itself struck more than 500 people, extending as far as Canada. Of those affected, at least six were reported to have died.

Strengthening the Chain

The food supply chain on which we all rely extends further and goes deeper than ever before. For example, a piece of fruit grown in Africa can be on grocery store shelves in Europe within 24 hours of harvest. Coffee from Asia wends its way to shops across Europe. Lamb from New Zealand is enjoyed across the UK [United Kingdom] and North America.

With such a far-reaching supply chain in place, carrying such an essential product as food, having the proper security and safety measures in place is vital.

The food supply chain on which we all rely extends further and goes deeper than ever before.

A robust, independently verified food management system could make a real difference by improving a food organization's flexibility, readiness and ultimate viability in the face of an ever-changing risk environment. This is particularly true when set against the backdrop of current economic pressures, when there is a temptation to cut corners. Under the circumstances, the need for food safety has never been greater. And yet, to this day, there has not been a unified, internationally accepted food safety management solution in place to do the job.

Good progress has been made by the industry to date. It was concern over potential risks in the food supply chain that prompted the creation of a number of early food safety sector initiatives and standards, including HACCP, [Hazard Analysis and Critical Control Points] and the BRC [British Retail Consortium] and IFS [International Food Standard] retailer-driven food manufacturing standards along with EuroGAP [European Good Agricultural Practices] for the pre-farm gate sector. But it was not until the publication of international food safety management system standard ISO [International Organization for Standardization] 22000 in 2005 that there was a single standard covering the entire food supply chain.

Adoption of ISO 22000 throughout all sectors of the industry has been relatively poor. In particular, in the highly influential food manufacturing sector, it quickly became apparent that ISO 22000 had limitations. From a technical perspective, the requirements on prerequisite programmes (PRPs) were not deemed to be specific enough to meet stakeholder needs.

Another limitation revolved around the position of the internationally recognized organization, the Global Food Safety Initiative (GFSI). Without the appropriate PRPs and scheme ownership, ISO 22000 could not be benchmarked by the GFSI and given the same approval as other standards.

Good progress has been made by the industry to date.

"The food safety landscape is very straightforward," says Steve Mould, worldwide quality management systems manager at Kraft Foods. "Food safety standards need to be recognized by the GFSI but ISO 22000 could not on its own. ISO 22000 gives lists of PRP topics to consider, but because it covers the whole of the food industry, it does not include PRPs for each step: otherwise it would need to be the size of an encyclopaedia. Something else was needed to fill the gap and give ISO 22000 the support that was needed."

Supporting Other Measures

Publicly Available Specification (PAS) 220 is a new complementary standard to ISO 22000. It has been designed to address the technical limitations around PRPs in ISO 22000 for the food manufacturing sector.

PAS 220:2008, prerequisite programmes on food safety for food manufacturing, was developed by BSI [British Standards Institution] and sponsored by Danone, Kraft Foods, Nestlé and Unilever through the Confederation of the Food and Drink Industries of the EU (CIAA). Other stakeholders involved in the development process included representatives from the Food and Drink Federation (FDF), McDonald's, General Mills Europe, and certification bodies.

FSSC 22000 (Food Safety System Certification 22000) is a new global food safety scheme which brings together ISO 22000 and PAS 220 certification for the food manufacturing industry.

"While existing schemes have a reasonable consistency of requirements, there was no true consistency of auditing and certification," says Mould, who was also the technical author of PAS 220. "Food safety schemes on the market today tend to be owned by stakeholders in the food supply chain. By moving to an independently owned certification scheme, we saw that we would be able to minimize system and audit variations based on geography, sector and customer, and reduce barriers to trade across the chain."

"An independent board comprising representatives from manufacturing, retail, consumer organizations and other international bodies is responsible for the content and management of FSSC 22000," says Cor Groenveld, chairman of the Foundation for Food Safety [Certification], the not-for-profit organization responsible for the scheme. "The scheme's independent ownership should make it attractive to all stakeholders."

Food Safety: A Public Health Priority

The availability of safe food improves the health of people and is a basic human right. Safe food contributes to health and productivity and provides an effective platform for development and poverty alleviation. People are becoming increasingly concerned about the health risks posed by microbial pathogens and potentially hazardous chemicals in food. Up to one-third of the populations of developed countries are affected by foodborne illness each year, and the problem is likely to be even more widespread in developing countries. The poor are the most susceptible to ill health. Food and waterborne diarrhoeal [diarrheal] diseases, for example, are leading causes of illness and death in less-developed countries, killing an estimated 2.2 million people annually, most of whom are children. Diarrhoea is the most common symptom of foodborne illness, but other serious consequences include kidney and liver failure, brain and neural disorders, and death. The debilitating long-term complications of foodborne disease include reactive arthritis and paralysis.

World Health Organization,
WHO Global Strategy for Food Safety, *2002.*

The scheme has been designed to meet the GFSI's benchmarking requirements and a decision by the GFSI board will take place in May 2009 as to whether FSSC 22000 is accepted as an approved certification scheme.

Cost Savings and New Opportunities

Once the GFSI approves FSSC 22000, Paul Whitehouse, quality manager at Unilever and another member of the PAS 220 steering group, believes one impact on the food manufacturing industry could be cost savings and new opportunities for SMEs [small and medium enterprises] and niche producers.

"Food safety is a destination; there are a number of routes and you choose one that best suits your organization," he says. "Given that companies are already used to working with ISO standards and are familiar with the risk and management systems based approach adopted by ISO 22000 and PAS 220, they may find it easier to align with these than with other standards."

"A GFSI-approved FSSC 22000 scheme could bring more food manufacturers into the fold, as well as encouraging other interested parties along the food chain to adopt similar PRP based approaches," says Joy Franks, the global product manager at BSI responsible for food safety.

We are heading towards a truly international food safety standard, one that covers the whole of the supply chain.

"The majority of the ISO 22000 certificates that have been issued to date come from outside the manufacturing sector," she says. "The driver was never there for manufacturers because of the PRP issues that are so central to their requirements. This has been addressed by ISO 22000 and PAS 220 and it's quite conceivable that, in a similar way, ISO 22000 plus new PAS 220 type standards could be used as a framework for other food sectors, for example retail, food service and packaging. If this was to become the case, then we'd have a more integrated approach to food safety management, which would be a great step forward for the industry and, ultimately, the consumer."

With seven of the world's largest supermarket chains already committed to accepting any scheme recognized by the GFSI, there is widespread optimism that FSSC 22000 will join the GFSI recognized list, says Groenveld: "The development of the scheme and PAS 220 has been a positive process, with international and broad industry input. Now we are just waiting for the GFSI approval and then we will hopefully see a significant impact in the industry."

"We are heading towards a truly international food safety standard, one that covers the whole of the supply chain" says Mould. "This will make the supply chain safer. If every aspect of the food industry adopted one international standard and operated under the same management system structure, then we will have more consistency and enhanced safety throughout the supply chain. With ISO 22000 and PAS 220 coming together under FSSC 22000, we're in a position for this to happen and we may well see a revolution in the food industry."

The European Union Sets Up an Agency for Food Safety

Chris White

In the following viewpoint, Chris White discusses the formation of the new European Union food protection agency (founded in January 2002). The European agency hopes to make its food hygiene regulations even more comprehensive than those of its counterpart in the United States. Food regulations are intended to be adhered to by member countries, applicant member countries, and countries exporting to the European Union. Chris White has been a contributing journalist for United Press International.

As you read, consider the following questions:

1. What measures does the European Union food protection agency hope to include as part of its ongoing work? What three countries are mentioned as exporting countries that would be affected by the new standards?
2. What would be the difference between the European and the American food agency standards?
3. Who is Phillip Whitehead, and what is his stand on the communication of food safety standards?

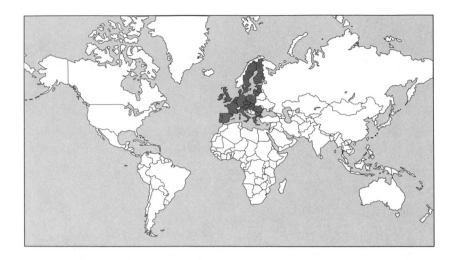

Brussels, Belgium, Jun 01, 2001 (United Press International via COMTEX)—Food producers around the world will have to meet exacting new hygiene standards set by the EU's new food safety agency if they want to export into its growing market.

Legislation to create the agency is on the fast track and has passed its first reading in the European Parliament, the EU's elected legislature in Brussels, and is on the agenda of the forthcoming summit meeting of EU government leaders in Gothenburg, Sweden.

Officials and members of the 626-member parliament are now forecasting "pre-emptive inspections" and "advice" to the rest of the world's food exporters, including those in the United States.

The agency, whose location has yet to be decided from among several competing European cities, is seen as a body that will progressively raise food hygiene standards throughout the European Union and in applicant member countries including Poland, Hungary and the Czech Republic.

A key difference between the United States, which introduced and set food hygiene standards, is that the EU takes the view that food hygiene regulations should cover production "from the farmyard to the table." The United States relies on chlorination or irradiation in the later stages of production.

The agency, whose location has yet to be decided from among several competing European cities, is seen as a body that will progressively raise food hygiene standards throughout the European Union and in applicant member countries including Poland, Hungary and the Czech Republic.

By creating a body that will set and raise Europe-wide standards, the EU will clarify the existing drafts of national legislation and will add legitimacy under world trade rules to its demands that exporters to Europe follow EU production practices.

The member of the European Parliament in charge of the agency bill, Phillip Whitehead (UK, Labor), says that the EU has not only a right but a duty to ensure that its standards are respected world wide.

"If, for example, in poultry production, we were taking certain measures to get rid of salmonella and for animal welfare reasons we were taking certain measures to make sure that there are not too many hens pushed into one cage, we have an absolute duty, I think, to communicate to the other countries outside the European Union, which produce for the European market, what we think their standards should be," he said Friday.

Saying that the agency should begin holding public hearings early next year he added that it must operational before the EU is enlarged.

"One of the important things we have got to remember in terms of timetable is that it should be in place well ahead of the process of accession by new member states. They have to understand that this is going to apply to them too and that food standards in the wider Europe are not going to be open to a period of derogation or whatever. We will need the same standards from everybody."

The existence of the new agency will strengthen the role of the EU's veterinary office based in Ireland.

"The office which looks after hygiene, sanitary and phytosanitary requirements, has not had the competence in the past to go to Brazil, say, to look at poultry or Thailand or somewhere like that and make pre-emptive inspections. What I think they will be able to do now is to go, at least on an advisory missions, and say to these countries that the standards prevailing in Europe ought to be observed by those who wish to export into Europe," Whitehead said.

"And I think, again, European consumers want to know because one of the consequences of globalization is that epidemics become ever more sweeping and terrifying. They become world-wide."

He stressed that the EU will set high standards for its own exports saying: "We want to see Europe saying the rest of the world is as deserving of our protection, as far as we can do it in the exports we send, as we are when those products are used in the European market."

Whitehead said: "The European Food Agency cannot just be a body that says Fortress Europa will do one thing, the rest of you foreigners can do what you like. It's got to be able to make certain that our standards are seen to be fair, not just protectionist and are seen to be things which can be linked to and followed up by producers elsewhere.

"And I think, again, European consumers want to know because one of the consequences of globalization is that epidemics become ever more sweeping and terrifying. They become world-wide."

China Deploys Radio Frequency Identification Technology to Ensure Food Safety

Tang Yuankai

In the following viewpoint Tang Yuankai, chief of the North American Bureau for the Beijing Review, *argues that China's recent implementation of radio frequency identification (RFID) tags will lead to a safer food supply. By attaching RFID tags to foods from seed to shelf, food safety inspectors will be able to ensure that the food is fresh and free from disease-causing agents. The Chinese RFID system will get its first major test at the Expo 2010 Shanghai China.*

As you read, consider the following questions:

1. In what year did China use RFID tags to track fish raised in Qiandao Lake?
2. What four basic parts are necessary for RFID tags to work effectively?
3. What are the three components of the RFID system?

Food safety inspectors will be tuning in to enforce the strict new food safety law that just came into force on June 1 [2009]. One of the tools they will rely on to get the job done

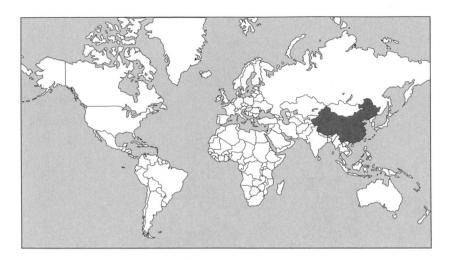

is in the form of radio frequency identification (RFID) tags, chips using radio waves to identify and track products.

RFID tags are used to replace the ubiquitous bar code system that requires contact or close proximity to work. RFID data can be read through the human body, clothing and nonmetallic materials. The tags can also be reused many times and can withstand heat and dirt.

The RFID tag's characteristics give it the upper hand over bar coding when tracking food production from raw materials and processing to transportation and storage. The information of the production chain associated with a piece of food can be recorded onto RFID tags, which can help to trace problems before consumption. Authorities hope this technology can help to build a better regulated food market.

In 2003, early in China's application of radio frequency technology to food tracking, the country attached RFID tags to fish raised in Qiandao Lake, Zhejiang Province. It was the first time China tagged fish products, which enabled customers and market administrators to track the food from water to table.

How RFID Systems Work

A basic RFID system needs four components to work: a transponder tag, a transceiver reader, an antenna attached to the reader and software that allows the tag to give its information to a computer.

The transponder tag holds unique identifying information. The transceiver reader emits and receives radio wave communication through its antenna and passes tag information to a computer attached to it.

The radio wave sent by the reader has the power to activate any tags nearby, which then emit their unique identifying information. The response is picked up by the antenna, sent to the reader and passed to the software that makes sense of it. The software, called middleware, can sort thousands of tag signals and makes it available on a computer for record keeping, analysis and management.

The RFID tag's characteristics give it the upper hand over bar coding when tracking food production from raw materials and processing to transportation and storage.

Besides product tracking, RFID is also used in passports, transportation payments and enterprise supply chain management to improve the efficiency of inventory tracking and management. RFID tags can be engineered as small as grains of powder, which makes them easy to conceal. Some tags can be read from several meters away and beyond the line of sight of the reader.

Revolutionizing the Expo

The world Expo 2010 Shanghai [China] will last 184 days and attract around 70 million visitors from more than 200 countries and regions. A paper co-authored by Wen Xuesong and Huang Guanwei of the Sino-German College [of Applied Sciences] at Shanghai-based Tongji University said food safety would be a major measurement of success for such a gigantic event. According to the authors, Shanghai should establish a food safety system consisting of monitoring, warning and emergency response, which covers the material production bases, processing plants and information management. The paper said RFID technology would play a vital role in this system.

To ensure the Expo's food safety, the paper said, a food production tracking system should be introduced to track food origins in a complicated multilayer supply network. The system supplied for the Expo should cover every step from production to consumption. "The adoption of RFID tags is an effective tool to track food origins since it can record point of production and every processing step. Thus we could track down the origins of all the foods sold at the Expo," wrote the paper.

The food supply chain is a complicated and multilayered dynamic system.

The paper said the Expo's daily food demands would change based on the number of visitors, their nationalities and the weather. Officials estimate that around 400,000 visitors will attend the Expo every day. "Using RFID tags will enable us to learn real-time food sales information, including the total sales and varieties," the paper stated. The authors said that on the one hand, the information could enable the Expo organizers to accurately stock retail outlets; on the other hand, the information could enable accurate food demand predictions, shorten supply cycles and cut down on food storage expenses. "The food supply chain using RFID technology that can respond quickly to customers' demands will bring services closer to visitors' actual demands and increase their overall trust and enjoyment while at the Expo," the paper said.

RFID Can Reduce Mistakes

Several years ago, genetically engineered corn was mistakenly sold as a standard hybrid. If RFID [radio frequency identification] was used to identify the field and grower, that data could be stored on an RFID tag on the truck carrying the seed from the field to the storage and processing facility. Reading this data could help prevent it from being loaded into the wrong silo. From there, rigorous internal quality controls, whether enabled by computer-controlled packaging equipment, bar codes or RFID on conveyances can then ensure proper packaging and identification. This would also provide traceability back to a specific field in the event of problems.

Bert Moore,
"RFID in the Food Chain: From Seed to Shelf,"
Association for Automatic Identification and Mobility,
August 2, 2007. www.aimglobal.org.

The food supply chain is a complicated and multilayered dynamic system, the authors wrote. Therefore, information integration holds the key to the efficient operation of the whole supply chain. In the traditional food supply chain, human errors made while collecting and checking product information can often lead to inaccuracies and lower work efficiency, making it impossible for information to be integrated along the whole food supply chain. The introduction of RFID technology has replaced traditional manual labor with automatic operations, substantially raising the efficiency and accuracy of information collection, reducing information loss during product transport, enhancing decision making while planning the food supply chain and providing the possibility of information integration.

Recording Important Information

The authors wrote that a supply system specially designed for the world Expo 2010 Shanghai [China] would use RFID tags to record food product information, including production, storage, transportation and sales data. Sales information on RFID tags can help managers to quickly adjust their delivery and storage volume and switch products between different retail outlets. Moreover, food safety can be guaranteed since the origin of every food item can be traced.

"Information control" serves as the central nervous system of the food supply.

"This system consists of three components—product flow, information flow and information control," the authors wrote, noting that "product flow" refers to the unidirectional flow of food products from producers to consumers. "Information flow" refers to the bidirectional data transmission accompanying "product flow," which enables producers to obtain accurate demand information and consumers to obtain food transportation information. "Information control" serves as the central nervous system of the food supply system and is in charge of receiving, analyzing and applying data collected by an RFID reader.

During food production and processing, an RFID tag will be affixed to every batch of raw materials during the transit from its source to a processing plant. Before the material is put onto the production line, every RFID tag will be scanned and basic information, like the place of origin and planting and harvesting times, will be read and stored in a database. The database can be used for future tracking if necessary. After going through production, a tag will once again be attached to the final product, which incorporates all the information from the raw materials as well as that from processing.

The products will be packaged and put on trays with RFID tags before being delivered or stored in a warehouse.

When being stored, products will have their RFID tags on trays scanned by an information system, which can obtain the storage history, destination and expiration date of every item or the entire package. The information system can automatically check in products and register information into the warehouse database. Moreover, the information system can accurately monitor the stockpile volume. When the volume drops close to or lower than the safety line, the system will automatically send out a reminder and an ordering plan matching the current shortages. The stockpile's manager will confirm the new order before it is sent out.

"The Beijing Olympics used tickets with RFID technology, which was a milestone in promoting China's RFID industry."

The paper stated that during food delivery, an information system would come up with a detailed replenishment plan for retail outlets according to their sales records. After the new replenishments arrive, their RFID tags will be scanned, which will transfer their information into the reserves database. Since tourists will change very fast, so will the structure of food purchases change. To avoid selling out a food item at one outlet, the information system can automatically send out warning messages when reserves drop below a certain level. Retail managers would be able to quickly arrange replenishment or call for transport of an item from one outlet to another.

Outlet clerks would scan information for products before putting them on shelves, the paper said. When selling food to customers, clerks would scan the RFID tags on products and on buyers' Expo tickets so that purchasing information could be recorded and the sales database could help to guarantee timely replenishment.

Smart Tickets

World Expo 2010 Shanghai [China] tickets will come with an embedded RFID tag to help eliminate counterfeit tickets and reduce the check-in time so that visitors do not have to wait in long queues.

The circuits in this new type of ticket record purchaser information and communicate wirelessly with transceivers installed across the Expo grounds. A network of connected computers can easily locate every visitor and even his or her companions from their tagged tickets. Once entering the Expo, visitors will receive an event map on their cell phones that will include other information like nearest bus stops and restaurants. Organizers can also inform visitors when venues are overcrowded so they can avoid those areas. Meanwhile, knowing the real-time distribution of visitors will also help organizers more efficiently direct traffic.

"The Beijing Olympics used tickets with RFID technology, which was a milestone in promoting China's RFID industry. We trust that it will become a trend for exhibitions and sports events to use tickets with electric chips, including RFID tags," said Li Rongxin, general manager of Shanghai Huahong Integrated Circuit Co. Ltd., the sole supplier of circuits for the Shanghai Expo tickets. In 1999, Huahong developed China's first non-touch integrated circuit (IC) card with its own proprietary rights. Bus passengers in Shanghai now use those cards. In 2004, the company was commissioned by the Ministry of Public Security to design circuits embedded in Chinese citizens' identity cards.

"RFID technology will soon be deployed in tickets to exhibitions, tourist spots and trains. This will give an enormous boost to the RFID industry's development in China by bringing in many opportunities," said Li.

China International Smart Cards and RFID Exhibition & Conference 2009 was held in Beijing in June. During this event, the IC Card Projects Coordination Office under the Central Government and RFID China Alliance jointly released a 2008 report on China's RFID industry development that predicted that the country's annual RFID market value in 2009 would surge by 20.6 percent to 7 billion yuan ($1 billion).

Self-Regulation by Food Companies Undermines Food Safety in Canada

Terry Pugh

Terry Pugh is the editor of the Union Farmer, *the journal of the National Farmers Union in Canada. In the following viewpoint, he asserts that allowing the food industry to regulate itself increases consumer health and safety risks. Pugh reports on the findings of Bob Kingston, a former inspector with the Canadian Food Inspection Agency (CFIA) and now head of the National Farmers Union. Kingston argues that the CFIA is not doing enough to ensure that food inspections are taken seriously and is now relying on the industry to catch and correct potentially serious code violations.*

As you read, consider the following questions:

1. Of the three thousand inspectors currently employed by the CFIA, how many of them are involved in food inspection?
2. According to Kingston, what percentage of time do inspectors spend inspecting food operations?
3. What percentage of the world food supply do large food companies such as Cargill and Louis Dreyfus control?

Terry Pugh, "Self-Regulation by Food Companies Undermines Food Safety," *CCPA Monitor*, vol. 15, April 2009, pp. 8–9. Copyright © 2009 CCPA. Reproduced by permission of Canadian Centre for Policy Alternatives, www.policyalternatives.ca.

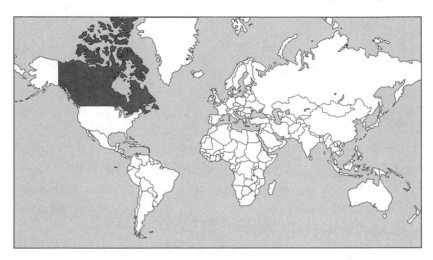

The listeriosis crisis that claimed the lives of at least 20 Canadians last summer and fall [2008] could have been prevented, according to the president of the agriculture union, a component of the Public Service Alliance of Canada (PSAC).

Bob Kingston told the annual convention of the National Farmers Union (NFU) that the deregulation of food safety inspections jeopardizes the health of Canadians.

The union, which represents food inspectors who work for the Canadian Food Inspection Agency (CFIA), launched a "Food Safety First" campaign last fall following the listeriosis outbreak. "The decision to go public wasn't taken lightly," said Kingston, "and was only made after federal Agriculture Minister Gerry Ritz began spreading misinformation about the situation."

The tragedy would not have happened if the government's plan to deregulate meat inspection had been in effect at the time.

Kingston said that prior to the listeriosis outbreak, a CFIA employee was fired for letting his union see a confidential letter that was sent by the federal Treasury Board to the CFIA.

"This letter outlined future [Prime Minister Stephen] Harper government plans to cut back on inspections in slaughter facilities," he said. "They were proposing to shift full-time meat inspection to just an oversight role."

Multiple Contradictions

Kingston said that when the listeriosis crisis first came to light, Ritz used the opportunity to claim that the tragedy would not have happened if the government's plan to deregulate meat inspection had been in effect at the time. The minister later went on to contradict himself, claiming that the inspection system had undergone no changes, that food inspectors spent only half their time doing physical inspections of products on the floor, and that an additional 200 inspectors had been hired by the CFIA.

"Unfortunately, all those statements were complete nonsense," said Kingston. "It turned out the minister had a real problem reading his briefing notes. The changes to the system were implemented in 2004 when the CFIA introduced a mandatory Hazard Analysis and Critical Control Points (HACCP) requirement for processing plants, including the Maple Leaf [Foods Inc.] plant in Toronto which was the source of the problem."

He added that the additional 200 inspectors were hired by the CFIA under the previous Liberal [Party] government through a program announced in 2005. They were hired not to do food inspections, but to work on a project to survey and eradicate foreign pests and diseases.

Out of the 3,000 inspectors currently employed by the CFIA nationwide, only 1,400 are actually involved in food inspection, and they are spread thinly across a large number of slaughter and processing plants.

"Last year, the Conservative [Party] government implemented what they called a 'Compliance Verification System,' which is a regimented approach to inspection," Kingston said.

"So, instead of focusing on areas in a plant where there are problems or speaking directly with workers on the plant floor, the inspectors are given a prescriptive list of inspection activities for that day, and are forbidden to stray from that specific list, regardless of what's going on around them."

Kingston said inspectors actually spend only about 25% of their time doing inspections in the plants, not 50% as claimed by the minister. A lot of the inspectors' time is taken up driving to and from the plants they are responsible for. He noted that the inspector assigned to the Maple Leaf plant in Toronto was also responsible for five other plants in the city, all of which have to be visited daily.

"It is physically impossible for one person to cover all those plants in an effective way," he said.

Self-Regulation

Kingston said the changes to the inspection system were brought in after much lobbying by the food industry to reduce government monitoring.

"Big business tends to see government inspection activities as simply slowing down the production process and reducing their profits," he said. "When the HACCP quality management systems were introduced in meat-processing plants, the large companies such as Maple Leaf argued that having these programs in place should mean less inspection, because they were now in a position to ensure compliance with health requirements on their own.

Inspectors have too much paperwork and too many facilities to cover to enable them to do effective inspections.

"Essentially we're talking about self-regulation. Many of these same companies were also asking for lower taxes and reduced government spending, and they found a sympathetic audience among many politicians. Under this corporate pressure, government departments, including the CFIA, were faced with program reviews and budget cuts and were receptive to any proposals that would result in less spending. This made them easy targets for industry lobbyists to get inspectors off the plant floor. The result is that processing inspectors are now in effect auditors who simply report how well the companies are performing under their own system, not under CFIA regulatory or policy requirements. So now, instead of taking some form of corrective action when they see problems, the inspectors just fill out a corrective action request and then they wait 10 days for the plant to tell them how they're going to fix the problem sometime in the next 60 days."

Kingston said the inspection system is "overburdened" because inspectors have too much paperwork and too many facilities to cover to enable them to do effective inspections.

"In the old days, the inspectors would have slowed down a production line until the problem was fixed. They would have had a chat with the foreman and they would have corrected the problem before they even left the plant. But that doesn't happen anymore. Instead of their conducting regular pre-operation or sanitation inspections, the plant employees now do these inspections themselves, with the CFIA inspectors reading about it when they get the time."

Under the old system, Kingston added, processing plants were automatically required to report positive Listeria finds to the inspector in charge, but under the new system that is no longer a requirement. "Some of the plants were not even aware that the requirement had been dropped, and even some of the inspectors weren't aware of it, but the big facilities, like Maple Leaf, which were the ones that lobbied for this new system—you better believe they knew it. There was a long history of positive Listeria finds, none of which were reported to an inspector. By the time the health authorities got hold of those samples, they were shocked by the amount of Listeria found in them, and by the number of samples that were contaminated."

The Profit Motive and Safety

Some observers still believe there is nothing wrong with food companies regulating themselves, given that it is so obviously in a company's best interests not to make their customers get sick or die. But Kingston said it is naïve to think the profit motive alone will guarantee safe food.

"Any inspector who has been around for a while can tell many stories that disprove that theory," he said. "If the profit motive caused businesspeople to act in their best long-term interests, we wouldn't have a worldwide banking crisis right now.

"The corporate agenda is about maximizing production volumes, production speed and profits, and unfortunately this often comes at the expense of quality and safety, and it also comes at the expense of workers and the viability of producers," Kingston said. "This is because big corporations have the political clout to write and rewrite the rules of the game, and their self-regulation maximizes their ability to achieve their goals, not ours. A handful of agribusiness companies like Cargill and Louis Dreyfus now control 80% of the world's food supply, and, like it or not, they didn't get there by looking out for the little guy."

The Australian Food Supply Is Vulnerable to Agroterrorist Attacks

Carl Ungerer and Dallas Rogers

In the following viewpoint, Carl Ungerer and Dallas Rogers, researchers in the School of Political Science and International Studies at the University of Queensland, Australia, argue that without significant improvements, the Australian food supply will remain vulnerable to attack by agroterrorists. A large-scale agroterrorist attack would not only cause significant physical harm to the people of Australia, but also greatly impact the country's economy. Therefore, the Australian government and the food industry must work together to protect the nation's food supply.

As you read, consider the following questions:

1. What percentage of Australia's annual gross domestic product does agriculture contribute?
2. What is contract calf-raising?
3. What are some crop pathogens that would cause major economic disruption in Australia?

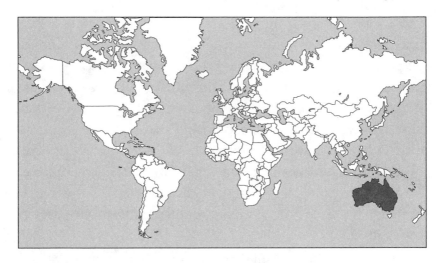

As in most Western countries, Australian intelligence agencies and policy makers have become increasingly concerned by the potential threat of terrorist attacks employing nonconventional weapons and methods. Much of the focus on this "new" terrorism has highlighted the potential use of weapons of mass destruction (WMD), comprising chemical, biological, radiological or nuclear (CBRN) weapons against civilian targets. The Australian Minister of Foreign Affairs and Trade, Alexander Downer, has described the threat from WMD terrorism as the "ultimate horror." Despite the political focus on WMD terrorism, however, less attention has been given to the threat of terrorist attacks against plant and animal populations in Australia. To date, the agricultural sector has not been considered an integral part of the public debate over critical infrastructure protection. Agricultural terrorism, or "agroterrorism," is defined as "the deliberate introduction of a disease agent, either against livestock or into the food chain, for purposes of undermining socioeconomic stability and/or generating fear." . . .

Agriculture Is Big Business

The Australian agricultural sector is one of the most viable in the world. Australia remains free of many exotic diseases that can cripple livestock industries and decimate crops. Agriculture contributes around 4 percent of Australia's gross domestic product (GDP) annually and a large share of Australia's exports. Attacks against this sector in Australia would cause significant economic harm to the country that in turn would have numerous flow-on effects within the Australian community. By addressing the importance of the Australian agricultural sector, and by illustrating the nature of contemporary Australian agribusiness practices, this section of the article outlines the extent of Australia's vulnerability to an agroterrorist attack.

Although most people understand that agriculture is a major industry in Australia, many would not be aware of the extent to which Australia depends on products, revenue, and employment in this sector. In 2002, there were over 135,000 establishments or businesses undertaking some form of agricultural activity in Australia. Within this group, a majority were engaged in beef/cattle farming (34,110), grain growing (15,911), mixed grain/sheep/beef farming (15,610), sheep farming (13,911), or dairy farming (11,135). The number of people directly employed by businesses within the agricultural sector stands at approximately 376,000. While this figure represents around 4 percent of the total labor force in Australia, the total number of people employed in related industries such as transport and food-processing plants would increase this figure to nearly 8.5 percent. Moreover, around 1 in 12 people depend on revenue earned from Australia's agricultural exports. It is clear that a terrorist incident resulting in the loss of employment for even a fraction of this population would have serious economic consequences for the Australian economy as a whole. A large-scale and purposeful agroterrorist attack could threaten the livelihood of many Australian families, as well as threaten the economic viability of some rural communities.

Australia's gross value of agriculture commodities stands at around $39.5 billion of which $11.4 billion comes from livestock slaughtering, $6.7 billion from livestock products, and $6.4 billion from wheat for grain alone. Wheat is Australia's largest crop, being produced in all states but concentrated in an area immediately inland from the Great Dividing Range along the east coast. Cattle, sheep, and pigs are the main livestock raised in Australia with the number of heads now standing at 27.8 million, 106.2 million, and 3.0 million, respectively. Cattle farming is conducted in all states and territories, whereas dairy farming is mainly restricted to the cooler, wetter areas of southern and coastal Australia. . . .

Dairy farming is performed in high rainfall coastal areas where, due to favorable conditions, it is possible to produce dairy products all year-round. In this industry, the use of feedlots and the supplementary use of grains as feed are becoming more common throughout Australia.

A large-scale and purposeful agroterrorist attack could threaten the livelihood of many Australian families.

Sheep and lamb farming is concentrated in Victoria and southern New South Wales as well as coastal border districts in southern South Australia. . . .

Pig and poultry farming are both highly intensive industries, with the majority of both being undertaken in large sheds to produce controlled and stable environments that are conducive to intensive animal husbandry techniques. Again, both pig and poultry farming [are] heavily concentrated in the southern states of New South Wales and Victoria.

Australia's Vulnerability to Agroterrorism

The geographic concentration of livestock production and farming in coastal and southern parts of Australia, which are climatically the coolest and wettest areas of the country, provides a favorable environment for the release of a foreign animal disease (FAD). In parts of Victoria, for example, the concentration of breeding animals at some farms is extremely high, which would further contribute to the ability of an agroterrorist to instigate an effective outbreak of infectious disease because of the high level of animal-to-animal contact that takes place. Also, the fact that all three major livestock animals susceptible to these types of diseases are concentrated in the southern regions of Australia means that a terrorist attack would most likely be executed in these areas, where a disease such as FMD [foot-and-mouth disease] could affect all three species—cattle, sheep, and pigs—simultaneously.

Farm security is an area of agribusiness that has received limited attention in Australia.

Agribusiness in Australia has changed significantly over the last 20 years. It is now much more intensive, with many large corporations consolidating farms to cut costs and increase both profit margins and competitiveness in international markets. The competition in consumer markets, both domestically and internationally, continues to drive prices down, forcing farmers to become more efficient in their farming practices. Like other Western countries, agricultural holdings in Australia generally follow an "80/20" rule, whereby 80 percent of the commodities are owned by the top 20 percent of companies. As a result, animal rearing has become a more concentrated, intensive, and highly technical business. Unfortunately, this places animals at greater risk of outbreaks of infectious diseases whether by an agroterrorist attack or by the accidental introduction of a disease. Moreover, to increase the quantity and quality of meat produced for the market, cattle are now subjected to higher stress levels, which in turn reduces their ability to overcome infection through immune response, leading to longer periods of infection and higher numbers of pathogens being shed in bodily secretions.

Although modern farming techniques such as contract calf-raising (where cattle are transported back and forth from farms designed to accelerate their growth) are not yet commonplace in Australia, growing pressure on agribusiness is resulting in its gradual introduction. Any technique that involves transporting livestock to different locations increases the probability that small clusters of disease will rapidly become major outbreaks at key focal points. In areas that practice contract calf-raising, young cattle could be reared on a particular farm, transported to larger feedlots for fattening, and then transported to slaughterhouses for processing, all within relatively short periods of time. Added to this is the huge distance that livestock can travel from their rearing yards to auction yards and then on to new owners' yards. In Australia, it is possible for livestock to travel long distances in a matter of three days, which is enough time to disguise an infected animal through the incubation period of the disease.

Most modern farms in Australia employ close feeding and watering conditions that provide a further mechanism for infectious agents to spread. Physical contact, increased exposure to fecal matter (which can be highly concentrated with pathogens), as well as the contamination of water and feeding troughs all ensure that FADs will spread quickly once introduced into a target population. As has been the case in various animal disease outbreaks in Europe, the movement of people and farming equipment is also a cause of widening disease outbreaks.

Farm security is an area of agribusiness that has received limited attention in Australia. Intensive livestock industries such as poultry and porcine exhibit relatively efficient security mechanisms, whereas the openness of cattle farms and feedlots suggests that unauthorized access to these animals would be extremely difficult to control or police. Security of auction yards is another vulnerability that could be exploited by an agroterrorist. Direct infection of a large number of animals could be possible either by inoculating the animals individually, or by placing animals that have been reared to spread the disease within the same enclosures as other auctioned animals.

Through quarantine and containment procedures, the Australian government has been broadly successful in preventing the accidental introduction of exotic foreign diseases. This has meant that Australia has remained "endemic-free" from most agricultural pathogens. However, a lack of previous exposure to these organisms, and therefore a lack of immunity, only increases the vulnerability of agricultural commodities to deliberate attack.

The capability requirements for [an] act of agroterrorism are much lower than for human bioterrorism attacks.

Agroterrorism Capability Requirements Are Low

The capability requirements for [an] act of agroterrorism are much lower than for human bioterrorism attacks. Information on infectious diseases that could be used as agroterrorist weapons is available on the Internet. Individuals with little or no training in microbiology or veterinary medicine can readily access information on the epidemiology, pathogenicity, and even disease diagnosis on many biological pathogens. Various Web sites provide detailed data regarding outbreaks of foreign animal and crop diseases, from which potential agroterrorists can acquire the location of epidemic and endemic areas. Added to this is the availability of online diagnostic images that illustrate the clinical symptoms associated with these particular diseases. As a result, a would-be agroterrorist has much of the information that he needs to acquire and control agricultural bioweapons.

International organizations such as the World Organisation for Animal Health (formerly known as the Office Inter-

Pathogens in Australia

Disease	Host range	Status
Foot-and-mouth disease (FMD)	Cloven-footed domestic and wild animals—cattle, sheep, pigs, etc.	Free
Vesicular stomatitis	Cattle, pigs, horses, humans	Free
Swine vesicular disease	Pigs	Free
Rinderpest	Cloven-footed domestic and wild animals—cattle, sheep, pigs, etc.	Free
Peste des petits ruminants	Goats, sheep	Free
Contagious bovine pleuropneumonia	Cattle	Free
Lumpy skin disease	Cattle	Free
Rift Valley fever (RVF)	Most animals—but mainly cattle, sheep, goats, humans	Free
Bluetongue	Sheep, cattle, goats	Virus present
Sheep pox and goat pox	Sheep and goats, respectively	Free
African horse sickness	Horses, mules	Free
African swine fever	Pigs	Free
Classical swine fever	Pigs	Free
Highly pathogenic avian influenza (HPAI)	Most avian species	Free
Newcastle disease	Poultry	Virus present

TAKEN FROM: Carl Ungerer and Dallas Rogers, "'Table: List A' Pathogens, Host Range, Status in Australia," *Studies in Conflict and Terrorism*, vol. 29, March/April 2006, p. 153. Copyright © 2006 Taylor & Francis Group, LLC. Reproduced by permission of Taylor & Francis, Ltd., http//:www.tandf.co.uk/journals and the authors.

national des Épizooties (OIE)) provide detailed lists of FADs that could cause significant socioeconomic or public health consequences, as well as the potential effect on international trade. . . . The OIE categorizes diseases based on the severity of their introduction to a "disease-free" area.

The diseases [noted by the OIE] would provide terrorists with weapons that would cause significant harm to primary-producing economies, especially to a country such as Australia. In recent years, the damage to agricultural industries in the United Kingdom and Southeast Asia from diseases such as FMD, bovine spongiform encephalopathy (BSE), and highly pathogenic avian influenza (HPAI) is an indication of the extent to which national economies can be affected by an outbreak of a FAD. These diseases are of concern to the Australian government for a variety of reasons: FMD because of the significant damage it would cause to the livestock industry and potential to become endemic; BSE because of its link to human disease; and HPAI because of its zoonotic nature. Both FMD and HPAI can be found in close proximity to Australian shores, shortening the amount of travel time an agroterrorist would require in order to import these diseases into Australia.

Although it is difficult to find a comprehensive list of crop pathogens, some that are mentioned as diseases that would cause major economic disruption to Australia are wheat rust, soybean rust, citrus greening, rice blast, and potato wart. Wheat rust is of particular concern, given the importance of the wheat industry to the overall national economy. The susceptibility of Australia's wheat crops has been recently highlighted by small outbreaks of the disease in northwestern New South Wales.

Ways of Obtaining Agricultural Pathogens

A terrorist intent on obtaining agricultural pathogens could do so in a number of ways. First, as mentioned previously, a terrorist could isolate an organism from the environment by tracking disease outbreaks. Many diseases of concern to Australia such as FMD, vesicular stomatitis, and rinderpest are endemic in less-developed countries geographically close to Australia. These diseases are widespread and many cases go unreported. Often, government control in these areas is ineffective, and most Southeast Asian countries lack the institutional and regulatory structures to control or eradicate these diseases. It is highly likely that the terrorist acquisition of infectious material from countries in Southeast Asia would go unnoticed by local authorities; FMD in the Philippines and HPAI throughout other parts of the Southeast Asian region are two pathogens that an agroterrorist could isolate with relative ease, and transport to Australia within a short period of time.

Second, terrorists could obtain the organism from a laboratory or biological collection agency where security is less stringent. Most Southeast Asian countries maintain hospital and university laboratories where stocks of biological pathogens are available. Security at many of these establishments remains less than adequate. A third and less likely possibility is that an organism suitable for an agroterrorist attack could be obtained from a state sponsor who shares a similar worldview as the terrorist group. Previous studies on WMD terrorism have tended to dismiss or downplay the possibility of states collaborating with terrorist groups because of the clear repercussions for any country seen to be assisting a terrorist organization in the acquisition or use of WMD. However, in the current climate, with numerous "rogue" states flouting nonproliferation norms, it would be imprudent to dismiss the possibility completely. Moreover, supplying biological agents to kill animals as opposed to humans is less likely to elicit a military response from the targeted state.

Bioweapons targeting agricultural commodities require little or no manipulation.

Port security remains a problem for preventing agroterrorism, as a recent case in New Zealand demonstrates. The biosecurity measures within New Zealand are generally considered to be world-class, and thought to be a highly effective deterrent against importing foreign biological material. However, in one case, farmers who had a long-running battle with government authorities over the problem of rabbits on their farms sought to isolate rabbit calicivirus from a foreign source, and infect the rabbit population within New Zealand. They were able to transport enough infectious material into the country to achieve their goals, illustrating the fallibility of existing biosecurity regimes. Indeed, the Australian Quarantine [and] Inspection Service (AQIS) shares many of the same procedures and policies as New Zealand with respect to concealed importation of biological material.

Unlike the inherent problems associated with weaponization of biological agents for a human bioterror attack, bioweapons targeting agricultural commodities require little or no manipulation. Many of the diseases mentioned earlier are highly contagious and can cause significant damage even from a single release point as was evident in the FMD outbreak in the United Kingdom. The low infective dose required for the disease to spread ensures that relatively little infectious material, perhaps as little as a few milliliters, would be needed to be transported to a target country in order to cause a significant outbreak. The non-zoonotic nature of most agricultural diseases also enables a terrorist to handle and transport FADs without any personal protective equipment that would be required if they were smuggling human pathogens. Attaching small "snap lock" bags to one's body, would allow an agroterrorist to import an agricultural pathogen into Australia with little or no difficulty.

A Potential Agroterrorism Scenario

In the context of this discussion it is prudent to ask: Exactly how would a terrorist group introduce a biological agent into the Australian agriculture sector for the purposes of a deliberate attack? This question has been underanalyzed in the literature on terrorist threats to Australia. The following provides a fictitious scenario that traces the simple steps needed to be taken by a terrorist group in order to conduct a successful act of agroterrorism using FMD.

To begin with, an individual or group would travel to an area where FMD is endemic, such as Thailand, Vietnam, or the Philippines and source the infectious material from selected animals. The organism could be gathered by swiping the lesions of an infected animal or by collecting the animal's saliva using a wet handkerchief. These small amounts of biological material could then be concealed in plastic bags and brought to Australia. Under the right conditions, the pathogen would remain active for much longer than the time it takes to travel to Australia. As body searches are not routinely employed by the Australian Quarantine [and] Inspection Service, the individuals would pass directly through Customs. Prior to, or perhaps concurrently, other persons would be involved in the purchase of livestock or a small farming operation in Australia. Because it is relatively easy to procure livestock animals in Australia, no record of such a small operation would be required. The infected material would be then used to inoculate the animals, allowing amplification of the agent over several days. Following significant amplification within a number of animals, transportation to a high-density livestock farming area would enable the terrorists to strategically place infected animals onto a number of farms, resulting in a significant multifocal point outbreak.

Although fictitious, the scientific credibility of this scenario is high. The ease at which agricultural pathogens can be found in the environment, the low infective dose needed, the vulnerabilities within agribusiness, and the effectiveness of diseases such as FMD make agroterrorism a real threat in Australia. The technical ease at which an agroterrorist attack could be perpetrated leads many foreign analysts to believe that if an attack was to occur, it would most likely begin in several locations simultaneously, overwhelming the response capacity of the authorities.

Food Safety and Security Remain Lacking in Sub-Saharan Africa

Donald G. Mercer

Donald G. Mercer is a professional engineer and associate professor in the Department of Food Science at the University of Guelph, Canada. In the following viewpoint, he argues that the food supply in sub-Saharan Africa continues to be unsafe. He cites unhygienic food storage, preparation, and disposal conditions and a lack of security at facilities as the main reasons for foodborne illnesses and economic losses in this vast region.

As you read, consider the following questions:

1. About what percentage of the world's food supply is lost due to spoilage?
2. Why are genetically modified crops considered to be superior to indigenous varieties?
3. What are some of the goals established by the United Nations Millennium Development Goals?

"Food security" can have different meanings to various people. To some, it means having an adequate supply of food material to feed the population of a country or region from one harvest period until the next. To others, the defini-

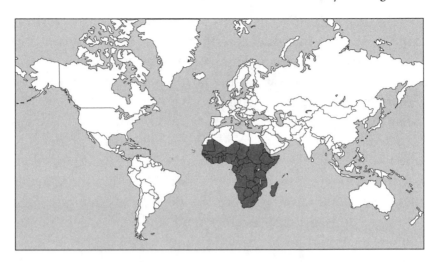

tion may vary somewhat and include safety and quality aspects such as the absence of physical, chemical, and biological contamination. There is also the fear of deliberate malicious acts involving a nation's food supply.

The United Nations Millennium Development Goals include reduction of hunger and poverty in developing countries of the world. Food safety and security are key components in this admirable quest.

The following is a brief examination of a number of aspects that contribute to food security, safety, and quality problems in developing countries, based on personal experience gained while on several assignments in sub-Saharan Africa.

A general lack of hygiene and overall cleanliness throughout the food supply chain has created conditions that can contribute to food spoilage and contamination.

Lack of Hygiene

A general lack of hygiene and overall cleanliness throughout the food supply chain has created conditions that can contribute to food spoilage and contamination. There is an awareness of HACCP (Hazard Analysis [and] Critical Control Points) among trained individuals within the agri-food sector, but there is little, if any, evidence of quality management programs being put in place at the farm level. It is not until food enters the commercial retail food chain that safety and quality seem to be a concern. Commercial food processors are making dedicated efforts to provide safe, high-quality products to their customers. However, the majority of the processed foods sold at retail are imported from countries with a more highly developed food industry. Since the majority of domestic food sales are done through local markets and at roadside stands, only a small portion of the food supply is influenced by these measures.

In many cases, products are transported from the farm to area markets by bicycle or even by bus.

Contamination of food may take place by physical, chemical, and/or biological means. There are ample opportunities for all of these to take place within the agri-food sector in sub-Saharan Africa. It is at the local markets and at the on-farm level where there is a tremendous need for improvement. It is not uncommon to see vendors spreading grain and other produce to dry on the bare earth or paved surfaces. The use of plastic sheeting placed under the food has been a major step forward in some areas.

On the farms, improper storage of chemical pesticides and herbicides in close proximity to finished products or animal feed can lead to chemical contamination of foods. The use of pesticides to kill rodents such as mice and rats provides another threat to human safety since the mice are often eaten and sold on skewers along the roadside. Physical contamination of food products with foreign materials may also occur due to lax storage conditions on the farm and throughout the supply chain.

Insects are also a major problem. Flies gather around roadside fruit and vegetable stands. They cluster on animal carcasses hung from wooden frames in the open air where merchants cut off slabs of meat with machetes for customers. In addition to insects, it does not take the visitor long to begin wondering about the threats of foodborne diseases such as trichinosis in pork.

The lack of a developed food transportation network and food handling system complicates the situation further. There is an alarming absence of refrigerated storage in many developing countries. There are few, if any, refrigerated trucks to deliver perishable products to retail outlets which in turn lack refrigeration capabilities. In many cases, products are transported from the farm to area markets by bicycle or even by bus.

Food Spoilage and Waste Handling

Food security also includes the loss of products due to spoilage. In the late 1980s, it was estimated by the World Health Organization that one-quarter to one-third of the world's food supply was lost due to spoilage before it reached the consumer. In tropical regions, losses were as high as 50%. Now, more than twenty years later, sources are still reporting postharvest losses of up to 50%. Cutting losses by half would have a significant impact on the ability of nations to feed themselves while reducing the dependence on food imports. Purchases of domestic products would also keep much-needed currency within a country to support the local economy rather than leaving the country to purchase imported foods.

Improved food processing and preservation facilities would go a long way in addressing such spoilage issues. In countries such as Equatorial Guinea, there are two growing seasons for tomatoes each year. During the "off-season", tomatoes are imported at a substantial cost. However, when the tomatoes are harvested, there are such large quantities available at such low prices that farmers receive a very poor return for their efforts. Within a few weeks, tomatoes are literally rotting on the vines in the fields and within a few more weeks, imported tomatoes are once again appearing in the markets. Due to a poorly developed infrastructure, abundant, reliable, and affordable electrical energy is unavailable to permit the establishment of a local food processing industry to produce shelf-stable tomato-based products.

Often spoiled fruits and vegetables and other unusable or unsalable products are simply dumped into a ravine or down the side of a hill.

Inadequate transportation networks including poor roads and bridges and an absence of specialty vehicles create a serious problem moving food products to distant commercial centers. The effects of vibration from poor roads, overloading of vehicles, and improper packing of loads are quite evident as vehicles deliver food products to local markets. The overall impact of spoilage and waste on a nation's food security cannot and should not be ignored.

Waste handling and disposal is not a very sophisticated process in many developing countries. Often spoiled fruits and vegetables and other unusable or unsalable products are simply dumped into a ravine or down the side of a hill. The garbage is then washed away by the rain and carried into streams and rivers, or contaminants are leached out of the refuse as the rainwater permeates through it. The net result is contamination of groundwater and drinking water sources, which creates additional health issues.

Waste heaps provide breeding grounds for vermin such as mice and rats, which in turn damage crops and stored food products, often rendering them unsafe for human consumption. Rotting garbage piles are also sources of disease spread by insects and rodents. Often the garbage is set on fire which creates an air pollution problem and a constant unpleasant odor. It is rather ironic that the food spoiled by rodents and insects gets discarded irresponsibly and itself becomes a source of further contamination by rodents and insects. There is a need to break into this vicious circle and address the rodent and insect problem. However, without proper waste-handling facilities and other necessary infrastructure, this is not happening in many areas.

Loss of indigenous varieties threatens food security at the basic genetic level and reduces the degree of biodiversity for future generations.

The Need for More Secure Facilities

Theft of food products from production facilities, warehouses, and primary production areas is a costly problem in terms of economic loss, but it also points to the vulnerability of food materials along the food supply chain. If food is not secure from theft, it is not secure from potential acts of malice. Such thefts also threaten the economic viability of farming and processing operations in countries which can ill afford such losses. Countries with scarce food resources are especially vulnerable to the effects of food theft on their citizens. In addition, conditions to which stolen food products are subjected before being illegally sold cannot be assumed to be the best for product quality and overall safety. Purchasers of these products are, therefore, putting themselves at risk.

At a cooperative in Malawi, thieves stole a large metal handle from the pump on the domestic water supply, rendering the pump unusable. This illustrates the deficiencies in security for both the water supply and the crops in some areas. Thefts from fields and orchards are also surprisingly frequent. There was one report of thieves entering macadamia nut plantations during the night and stealing large quantities of this high-value product. The scale of these thefts would require a

Principal Marketing and Distribution Channels for Fresh Fruit, Vegetables, and Root Crops

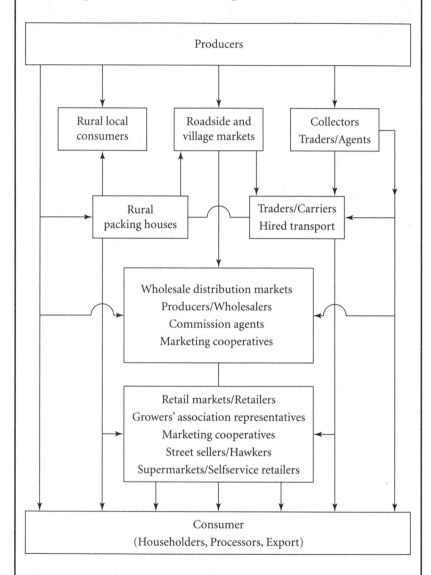

TAKEN FROM: Food and Agriculture Organization of the United Nations, "Prevention of Post-Harvest Food Losses, Fruits, Vegetables, and Root Crops: A Training Manual," 1989.

considerable number of individuals to harvest the nuts. Government officials who raided the homes of the suspected thieves found what was described as huge quantities of macadamia nuts stored in bags awaiting shipment out of the country.

Genetically modified crops are frequently considered to be superior to indigenous varieties. Having been bred for drought tolerance or insect resistance, they offer farmers enhanced yields with lower input costs. Herbicide-resistant crops reduce the number of applications of specific weed killers throughout the growing season which once again adds to the attractiveness of genetically modified hybrids. For these reasons, genetically modified varieties have often replaced lower-yielding indigenous varieties which may have been used for generations prior to the advent of the biotechnology revolution. While traditional local varieties may be preferred for their taste, texture, and other properties, there is an inherent reluctance or unwillingness on the part of the consumer to pay premium prices to compensate for lower yields. In the struggle for economic survival, many farmers have abandoned these varieties in favor of more profitable crops. Loss of indigenous varieties threatens food security at the basic genetic level and reduces the degree of biodiversity for future generations.

Spoilage and issues associated with food security are not only limited to the food material itself. There are additional social and economic implications that need to be kept in mind. Accompanying a 25% loss in food due to spoilage is the associated loss of labor and energy inputs as well as the generation of wastes and pollutants for little or no commercial value. Fertilisers and irrigation water used to grow this food are essentially wasted, as are the transportation, storage, and other distribution costs required to move food from its point of origin to its points of sale and consumption. Using a food chain management approach will do much to address these problems and will hopefully make more high-quality food available to those who need it the most.

During a recent assignment in sub-Saharan Africa, several individuals related accounts of breaches of food safety. In spite of the fact that this is secondhand information or hearsay evidence, the adage "where there is smoke, there is fire" would seem appropriate. According to these sources, some chicken farmers have been adding human birth control pills to the rations fed to their flocks to enhance growth rates and thereby reduce the time taken to bring their birds to a marketable weight. There is little concern on their part regarding the effects of elevated levels of estrogen on the consumer. Additional stories were told about the use of unsafe chemicals being added to meats and meat products to enhance their shelf life. It was also stated that mosquito nets saturated with pyrethrums were being used for fishing. These nets were originally intended to reduce malaria and were provided by international aid organisations. The pyrethrums are potential potent water pollutants that can then enter the human food chain.

The problems in sub-Saharan Africa are so vast due to the number of people and the geographical area that it is difficult to make the desired level of progress.

While there is no concrete evidence to back up these "stories", their very existence is alarming. A more in-depth examination of the safety of the food supply chain in developing nations would seem to be warranted to either substantiate or dispel these "rumors". Measures would then be required to alleviate these undesirable practices.

Improvements Have Been Made

There have been many advances in promoting food safety and security in developing nations within sub-Saharan Africa. International aid organizations working closely with national governments or regional bodies have devoted considerable attention to bringing safe drinking water to many areas. This is a key step in the reduction of disease. Improved farming practices and higher-yielding crops with additional benefits such as drought resistance have increased productivity and have contributed to improved nutrition and quality of life. However, the problems in sub-Saharan Africa are so vast due to the number of people and the geographical area that it is difficult to make the desired level of progress. The United Nations Millennium Development Goals have targeted reductions in poverty and hunger by 2015. We are more than halfway to this deadline since these goals were established and by many accounts there is still a long way to go before these objectives are reached.

Anyone who has travelled to this part of the world will have his or her own personal experiences upon which to re flect. Those living in any of the more than forty nations that comprise this region will have a much deeper insight than a paper of this nature can ever hope to provide.

Those of you with children know all too well the familiar phrase "Are we there yet?" which is shouted out soon after any journey begins. In the case of food safety and security in many African nations, the unfortunate answer is, "No". It is even more disturbing to see how little ground has been covered and how far we still have to go before we reach this important objective. By working together and directing our collective energies to such critical issues as food safety and security, progress will be made—the problem lies in speeding up the process and reaching out to the millions of people who are in need of assistance.

Periodical Bibliography

The following articles have been selected to supplement the diverse views presented in this chapter.

Sylvain Charlebois — "More Regulation Doesn't Buy Less Risk; Supply Chain Management," *Financial Post* (Canada), October 28, 2008.

Paul Cullen — "Food Safety Breaches Rise 17% with 34 Closures," *Irish Times*, January 9, 2010.

Kari Tove Elvbakken, Per Lægreid, and Lise Hellebø Rykkja — "Regulation for Safe Food: A Comparison of Five European Countries," *Scandinavian Political Studies*, June 2008.

Moritz Hagenmeyer — "Legal Requirements for the Production of Safe Food: A Brief Outline of the Most Important Legal Provisions to Be Observed by Food Business Operators in Order to Achieve Food Safety," *European Food and Feed Law Review*, vol. 4, no. 5, 2009.

Korea Times — "Global Experts to Explore Ways to Enhance Food Safety," January 13, 2009.

Wang Qian — "National Safety System to Push Tainted Food off Shelves," Chinadaily.com.cn, June 13, 2009. www.chinadaily.com.cn.

Lesley Russell — "Call for Action on Food Safety," *Canberra Times* (Australia), July 14, 2009.

Yali Tang, Lixin Lu, Wei Zhao, and Jun Wang — "Rapid Detection Techniques for Biological and Chemical Contamination in Food: A Review," *International Journal of Food Engineering*, vol. 5, no. 5, 2009.

Beck Vass — "Ministry Says Amended Food Bill Will Not Improve Safety," *New Zealand Herald*, October 23, 2009.

CHAPTER 2

Food Scarcity and Security

Running Out of Oil Will Cause a Global Food Shortage

Richard Heinberg

Richard Heinberg is the author of Powerdown: Options and Actions for a Post-Carbon World *and a core faculty member of New College of California. In the following viewpoint, he argues that running out of oil and other fossil fuels will devastate the world's food supply. Humans currently rely on these sources of energy to produce, process, and ship food. Unless the world moves toward other means of feeding its people, real starvation and related catastrophes are imminent.*

As you read, consider the following questions:

1. How many gallons of oil are needed to feed one American each year?

2. What percentage of the earth's primary biological productivity are humans currently using?

3. On average, how many pounds did Cubans lose during the food crisis in the 1990s?

In the US [United States], agriculture is directly responsible for well over 10 percent of all national energy consumption. Over 400 gallons of oil equivalent are expended to feed each American each year. About a third of that amount goes to-

Richard Heinberg, "What Will We Eat as the Oil Runs Out?" FEASTA Conference, Dublin, Ireland, June 23–25, 2005. Reproduced by permission of Richard Heinberg, Senior Fellow of Post Carbon Institute. http://www.postcarbon.org.

ward fertilizer production, 20 percent to operate machinery, 16 percent for transportation, 13 percent for irrigation, 8 percent for livestock raising (not including the feed), and 5 percent for pesticide production. This does not include energy costs for packaging, refrigeration, transportation to retailers, or cooking.

Trucks move most of the world's food, even though trucking is ten times more energy intensive than moving food by train or barge. Refrigerated jets move a small but growing proportion of food, almost entirely to wealthy industrial nations, at 60 times the energy cost of sea transport.

Processed foods make up three-quarters of global food sales by price (though not by quantity). This adds dramatically to energy costs: For example, a one-pound box of breakfast cereal may require over 7,000 kilocalories of energy for processing, while the cereal itself provides only 1,100 kilocalories of food energy.

Overall—including energy costs for farm machinery, transportation, and processing, and oil and natural gas used as feedstocks for agricultural chemicals—the modern food system consumes roughly ten calories of fossil fuel energy for every calorie of food energy produced.

There is growing debate over the question of how to avoid an agricultural Armageddon.

But the single most telling gauge of our dependency is the size of the global population. Without fossil fuels, the stupendous growth in human numbers that has occurred over the past century would have been impossible. Can we continue to support so many people as the availability of cheap oil declines?

Feeding a Growing Multitude

The problems associated with the modern global food system are widely apparent; there is widespread concern over the sustainability of the enterprise, and there is growing debate over the question of how to avoid an agricultural Armageddon. Within this debate two viewpoints have clearly emerged.

The first advises further intensification of industrial food production, primarily via the genetic engineering of new crop and animal varieties. The second advocates ecological agriculture in its various forms—including organic, biodynamic, permaculture, and biointensive methods.

Critics of the latter contend that traditional, chemical-free forms of agriculture are incapable of feeding the burgeoning human population. Here is a passage by John Emsley of the University of Cambridge, from his review of Vaclav Smil's *Enriching the Earth: Fritz Haber, Carl Bosch, and the Transformation of World Food Production*:

> If crops are rotated and the soil is fertilized with compost, animal manure and sewage, thereby returning as much fixed nitrogen as possible to the soil, it is just possible for a hectare of land to feed 10 people—provided they accept a mainly vegetarian diet. Although such farming is almost sustainable, it falls short of the productivity of land that is fertilized with "artificial" nitrogen; this can easily support 40 people, and on a varied diet.

The bioengineering of crop and animal varieties does little or nothing to solve this problem.

This seems unarguable on its face. However, given the fact that fossil fuels are nonrenewable, it will be increasingly difficult to continue to supply chemical fertilizers in present quantities. Nitrogen can be synthesized using hydrogen produced from the electrolysis of water, with solar or wind power as a source of electricity. But currently no ammonia is being commercially produced this way because of the uncompetitive cost of doing so. To introduce and scale up the process will require many years and considerable investment capital.

The bioengineering of crop and animal varieties does little or nothing to solve this problem. One can fantasize about modifying maize or rice to fix nitrogen in the way that legumes do, but so far efforts in that direction have failed. Meanwhile, the genetic engineering of complex life forms on a commercial scale appears to pose unprecedented environmental hazards, as has been amply documented by Dr. Mae-Wan Ho among many others. And the bioengineering industry itself consumes fossil fuels and assumes the continued availability of oil for tractors, transportation, chemicals production, and so on.

We must turn to a food system that is less fuel reliant, even if it does prove to be less productive.

Supporting Ecoagriculture

Those arguing in favor of small-scale, ecological agriculture tend to be optimistic about its ability to support large populations. For example, the 2002 Greenpeace report *The Real Green Revolution: Organic and Agroecological Farming in the South*, while acknowledging the lack of comparative research on the subject, nevertheless notes:

> In general . . . it is thought that [organic and agroecological farming] can bring significant increases in yields in comparison to conventional farming practices. Compared to "Green Revolution" farming systems, OAA [organic and agroecological approaches] is thought to be neutral in terms of yields, although it brings other benefits, such as reducing the need for external inputs.

Ecoagricultural advocates often contend that there is plenty of food in the world; existing instances of hunger are due to bad policy and poor distribution. With better policy and distribution, all could easily be fed. Thus, given the universally admitted harmful environmental consequences of conventional chemical farming, the choice should be simple.

Agriculture Energy Consumption

In the United States, 400 gallons of oil equivalents are expended annually to feed each American (as of data provided in 1994). Agricultural energy consumption is broken down as follows:

- 31% for the manufacture of inorganic fertilizer
- 19% for the operation of field machinery
- 16% for transportation
- 13% for irrigation
- 08% for raising livestock (not including livestock feed)
- 05% for crop drying
- 05% for pesticide production
- 08% miscellaneous

Energy costs for packaging, refrigeration, transportation to retail outlets, and household cooking are not considered in these figures.

Dale Allen Pfeiffer,
"Eating Fossil Fuels," 2004.
www.fromthewilderness.com.

Some eco-ag proponents are even more sanguine, and suggest that their methods can produce far higher yields than can mechanized, chemical-based agriculture. Experiments have indeed shown that small-scale, biodiverse gardening or farming can be considerably more productive on a per-hectare basis than monocropped megafarms. However, some of these studies have ignored the energy and land-productivity costs of manures and composts imported onto the study plots. In any case, and there is no controversy on this point, permaculture and biointensive forms of horticulture are dramatically more labor—and knowledge—intensive than industrial agriculture. Thus the adoption of these methods will require an economic transformation of societies.

Therefore even if the nitrogen problem can be solved in principle by agroecological methods and/or hydrogen production from renewable energy sources, there may be a carrying-capacity bottleneck ahead in any case, simply because of the inability of societies to adapt to these very different energy and economic needs quickly enough, and also because of the burgeoning problems mentioned . . . (loss of freshwater resources, unstable climate, etc.). According to widely accepted calculations, humans are presently appropriating at least 40 percent of Earth's primary biological productivity. It seems unlikely that we, a single species after all, can do much more than that. Even though it may not be politically correct in many circles to discuss the population problem, we must recognize that we are nearing or past fundamental natural limits, no matter which course we pursue.

Given the fact that fossil fuels are limited in quantity and we are already in view of the global oil production peak, the debate over the potential productivity of chemical-gene engineered agriculture versus that of organic and agroecological farming may be relatively pointless. We must turn to a food system that is less fuel reliant, even if it does prove to be less productive.

The Example of Cuba

How we might do that is suggested by perhaps the best recent historical example of a society experiencing a fossil fuel famine. In the late 1980s, farmers in Cuba were highly reliant on cheap fuels and petrochemicals imported from the Soviet Union, using more agrochemicals per acre than their American counterparts. In 1990, as the Soviet empire collapsed,

Cuba lost those imports and faced an agricultural crisis. The population lost 20 pounds on average and malnutrition was nearly universal, especially among young children. The Cuban GDP [gross domestic product] fell by 85 percent and inhabitants of the island nation experienced a substantial decline in their material standard of living.

Cuban authorities responded by breaking up large state-owned farms, offering land to farming families, and encouraging the formation of small agricultural co-ops. Cuban farmers began employing oxen as a replacement for the tractors they could no longer afford to fuel. Cuban scientists began investigating biological methods of pest control and soil fertility enhancement. The government sponsored widespread education in organic food production, and the Cuban people adopted a mostly vegetarian diet out of necessity. Salaries for agricultural workers were raised, in many cases to above the levels of urban office workers. Urban gardens were encouraged in parking lots and on public lands, and thousands of rooftop gardens appeared. Small food animals such as chickens and rabbits began to be raised on rooftops as well.

As a result of these efforts, Cuba was able to avoid what might otherwise have been a severe famine. Today the nation is changing from an industrial to an agrarian society. While energy use in Cuba is now one-twentieth of that in the US, the economy is growing at a slow but steady rate. Food production has returned to 90 percent of its precrisis levels.

The Way Ahead

The transition to a non–fossil fuel food system will take time. And it must be emphasized that we are discussing a systemic transformation—we cannot just remove oil in the forms of agrochemicals from the current food system and assume that it will go on more or less as it is. Every aspect of the process by which we feed ourselves must be redesigned. And, given the likelihood that global oil peak will occur soon, this transition must occur at a rapid pace, backed by the full resources of national governments.

Without cheap transportation fuels we will have to reduce the amount of food transportation that occurs, and make necessary transportation more efficient. This implies increased local food self-sufficiency. It also implies problems for large cities that have been built in arid regions capable of supporting only small populations on their regional resource base. One has only to contemplate the local productivity of a place like Nevada to appreciate the enormous challenge of continuing to feed people in a city such as Las Vegas without easy transportation.

Every aspect of the process by which we feed ourselves must be redesigned.

We will need to grow more food in and around cities. Currently, Oakland, California, is debating a food policy initiative that would mandate by 2015 the growing within a fifty-mile radius of city center of 40 percent of the vegetables consumed in the city. If the example of Cuba were followed, rooftop gardens would result, as well as rooftop raising of food animals like chickens, rabbits and guinea pigs.

Localization of the food process means moving producers and consumers of food closer together, but it also means relying on the local manufacture and regeneration of all of the elements of the production process—from seeds to tools and machinery. This would appear to rule out agricultural bioengineering, which favors the centralized production of patented seed varieties, and discourages the free saving of seeds from year to year by farmers.

Clearly, we must minimize chemical inputs to agriculture (direct and indirect—such as those introduced in packaging and processing).

We will need to reintroduce draft animals in agricultural production. Oxen may be preferable to horses in many instances, because the former can eat straw and stubble, while the latter would compete with humans for grains.

Government Policies

Governments must also provide incentives for people to return to an agricultural life. It would be a mistake simply to think of this simply in terms of the need for a larger agricultural workforce. Successful traditional agriculture requires social networks and intergenerational sharing of skills and knowledge. We need not just more agricultural workers, but a rural culture that makes agricultural work rewarding.

Farming requires knowledge and experience, and so we will need education for a new generation of farmers; but only some of this education can be generic—much of it must of necessity be locally appropriate.

It will be necessary as well to break up the corporate mega-farms that produce so much of today's cheap grain. Industrial agriculture implies an economy of scale that will be utterly inappropriate and unworkable for postindustrial food systems. Thus land reform will be required in order to enable smallholders and farming co-ops to work their own plots.

We need not just more agricultural workers, but a rural culture that makes agricultural work rewarding.

In order for all of this to happen, governments must end subsidies to industrial agriculture and begin subsidizing postindustrial agricultural efforts. There are many ways in which this could be done. The present regime of subsidies is so harmful that merely stopping it in its tracks might in itself be advantageous; but, given the fact that a rapid transition is essential, offering subsidies for education, no-interest loans for land purchase, and technical support during the transition from chemical to organic production would be essential.

Finally, given carrying-capacity limits, food policy must include population policy. We must encourage smaller families by means of economic incentives and improve the economic and educational status of women in poorer countries.

All of this constitutes a gargantuan task, but the alternatives—doing nothing or attempting to solve our food-production problems simply by applying more technological intensification—will almost certainly result in dire consequences. In that case, existing farmers would fail because of fuel and chemical prices. All of the worrisome existing trends . . . would intensify to the point that the human carrying capacity of Earth would be degraded significantly, and perhaps to a large degree permanently.

In sum, the transition to a fossil fuel–free food system does not constitute a utopian proposal. It is an immense challenge and will call for unprecedented levels of creativity at all levels of society. But in the end it is the only rational option for averting human calamity on a scale never before seen.

Climate Change and Overharvesting Are Reducing the World's Fish Supply

Christian Nellemann, Stefan Hain, and Jackie Alder

In the following viewpoint, Christian Nellemann, Stefan Hain, and Jackie Alder, researchers for the United Nations Environment Programme, argue that the world's oceans and their inhabitants are in distress. They cite global climate change and pollution as key factors in this destruction. They also point to overharvesting and aggressive fishing methods as contributing to the disruption of oceanic ecosystems. They argue that urgent action is needed to prevent what appears to be an impending food supply catastrophe.

As you read, consider the following questions:

1. By what percentage are the world's coral reefs expected to be bleached by 2080?
2. What percentage of marine pollution originates from land-based sources?
3. By how many did the number of dead zones increase between 2003 and 2006?

Christian Nellemann, Stefan Hain, and Jackie Alder, *In Dead Water: Merging of Climate Change with Pollution, Over-Harvest, and Infestations in the World's Fishing Grounds*, Arendal, Norway: United Nations Environment Programme/GRID-Arendal, 2008, pp. 7–12. Reproduced by permission.

The world's oceans play a crucial role for life on the planet. Healthy seas and the services they provide are key to the future development of mankind. Our seas are highly dynamic, structured and complex systems. The seafloor consists of vast shelves and plains with huge mountains, canyons and trenches which dwarf similar structures on land. Ocean currents transport water masses many times larger than all rivers on Earth combined.

In this [viewpoint], the locations of the most productive fishing grounds in the world—from shallow, coastal waters to the deep and high seas—are compared to projected scenarios of climate change, ocean acidification, coral bleaching, intensity of fisheries, land-based pollution, increase of invasive species infestations and growth in coastal development.

Half the world catch is caught in less than 10% of the ocean.

There are alarming signals that these natural processes to which marine life is finely attuned are rapidly changing.

Marine life and living resources are neither evenly nor randomly distributed across the oceans. The far largest share of marine biodiversity is associated with the seabed, especially on the continental shelves and slopes. Seamounts, often rising several thousand meters above their surroundings, provide unique underwater oases that teem with life. Environmental parameters and conditions that determine the productivity of the oceans vary greatly at temporal and spatial scales. The primary and most important fishing grounds in the world are found on and along continental shelves within less than 200 nautical miles of the shores. The distribution of these fishing grounds is patchy and very localized. Indeed more than half of the 2004 marine landings are caught within 100 km [kilometers] of the coast with depths generally less than 200 m [meters] covering an area of less than 7.5% of the world's oceans, and 92% in less than half of the total ocean area. These treasure vaults of marine food play a crucial role for coastal populations, livelihoods and the economy.

Whether they will provide these functions and services in the future depends on needed policy changes and the continuation of a number of environmental mechanisms to which marine life has evolved and adapted. These natural processes include clean waters with balanced temperature and chemistry regimes as well as currents and water exchanges that provide these areas with oxygen and food, to name just a few. However, there are alarming signals that these natural processes to which marine life is finely attuned are rapidly changing.

Alarming Signals

With climate change, more than 80% of the world's coral reefs may die within decades.

In tropical shallow waters, a temperature increase of up to only 3 °C [Celsius] . . . may result in annual or biannual bleaching events of coral reefs from 2030–2050. Even the most optimistic scenarios project annual bleaching in 80–100% of the world's coral reefs by 2080. This is likely to result in severe damage and widespread death of corals around the world, particularly in the Western Pacific, but also in the Indian Ocean, the Persian Gulf and the Middle East and in the Caribbean.

Ocean acidification will also severely damage cold-water coral reefs and affect negatively other shell-forming organisms.

As CO_2 [carbon dioxide] concentrations in the atmosphere increase so does ocean assimilation, which, in turn, results in seawater becoming more acidic. This will likely result in a reduction in the area covered and possible loss of cold-water coral reefs, especially at higher latitudes. Besides cold-water corals, ocean acidification will reduce the biocalcification of other shell-forming organisms such as calcareous phytoplankton, which may in turn impact the marine food chain up to higher trophic levels.

Coastal development is increasing rapidly and is projected to impact 91% of all inhabited coasts by 2050 and will contribute to more than 80% of all marine pollution.

Marine pollution, more than 80% of which originates from land-based sources, is projected to increase, particularly in Southeast and East Asia, due to rising population and coastal development. Increased loads of sediments and nutrients from deforestation, sewage and river runoff will greatly diminish the resilience of coral reefs. The effects of pollution are exacerbated by the destruction of mangroves and other habitats due to the rapid construction taking place on coastlines. As much as 91% of all temperate and tropical coasts will be heavily impacted by development by 2050. These impacts will be further compounded by sea level rise and the increased frequency and intensity of storms that easily break down weakened or dead corals and are likely to severely damage beaches and coastlines.

Climate change may slow down ocean thermohaline circulation and continental shelf "flushing and cleaning" mechanisms crucial to coastal water quality and nutrient cycling and deepwater production in more than 75% of the world's fishing grounds.

The effects of pollution are exacerbated by the destruction of mangroves and other habitats due to the rapid construction taking place on coastlines.

Increasing Dead Zones

Of major concern is that many of these productive fishing grounds depend extensively upon sea currents for maintaining life cycle patterns for the sustainable production of fish and other marine life. Large-scale water exchange mechanisms, which periodically "flush and clean" continental shelf areas, are observed in and near at least 75% of all the major fishing grounds. These mechanisms, however, depend entirely on cooler and heavier seawater sinking into the deep sea, often using and carving channels and canyons into the continental shelf. New research suggests that while climate change may not necessarily stop the major thermohaline currents, climate change may potentially reduce the intensity and frequency of the coastal flushing mechanisms, particularly at lower to medium latitudes over the next 100 years, which in turn will impact both nutrient and larval transport and increase the risk of pollution and dead zones.

Increased development, coastal pollution and climate change impacts on ocean currents will accelerate the spreading of marine dead zones, many around or in primary fishing grounds.

The number of dead zones (hypoxic or oxygen deficient areas) increased from 149 in 2003 to over 200 in 2006. Given their association with pollutants from urban and agricultural sources, together with the projected growth in coastal development, this number may multiply in a few decades, unless substantial changes in policy are implemented. Most dead zones, a few of which are natural phenomena, have been observed in coastal waters, which are also home to the primary fishing grounds.

Trawling has been estimated to be as damaging to the seabed as all other fishing gear combined.

Overharvesting and Bottom Trawling

Overharvesting and bottom trawling are degrading fish habitats and threatening the entire productivity of ocean biodiversity hot spots, making them more vulnerable to climate change.

The World's Most Productive Fishing Grounds

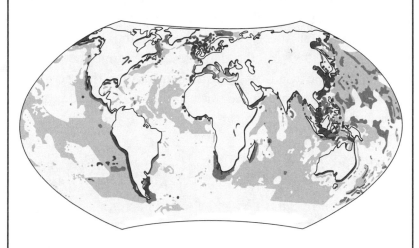

Fish catch (2004) tonnes/km²

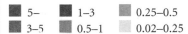

■ 5– ■ 1–3 ▨ 0.25–0.5
■ 3–5 ■ 0.5–1 ▨ 0.02–0.25

Caption: The World's most productive fishing grounds are confined to major hotspots, less than 10% of the World's oceans. The map shows annual catch (tonnes per km²) for the World's oceans. Notice the strong geographic concurrence of continental shelves, upwelling and primary productivity and the amount of fish caught by fisheries.

TAKEN FROM: Christian Nellemann, Stefan Hain, and Jackie Alder, *In Dead Water: Merging of Climate Change with Pollution, Over-Harvest, and Infestations in the World's Fishing Grounds*, Arendal, Norway: United Nations Environment Programme/GRID-Arendal, 2008. Reproduced by permission.

Recent studies indicate that fishery impacts in shelf areas may potentially become even worse in deeper water. Due to advances in technology and subsidies, fishing capacity is now estimated to be as much as 2.5 times that needed to harvest the sustainable yield from the world's fisheries. Up to 80% of the world's primary catch species are exploited beyond or close to their harvest capacity, and some productive seabeds have been partly or even extensively damaged over large areas of fishing grounds. With many traditional, shallow fishing grounds depleted, fisheries (especially large industrial vessels/ fleets operating for weeks/months at sea) are increasingly targeting deepwater species on the continental slopes and seamounts. Over 95% of the damage and change to seamount ecosystems is caused by bottom fishing, mostly carried out unregulated and unreported with highly destructive gear such as trawls, dredges and traps.

Heavily disturbed and damaged marine areas are more likely to have a higher vulnerability to infestations brought in by ships plying the world's oceans.

Trawling has been estimated to be as damaging to the seabed as all other fishing gear combined. Unlike only a decade ago, there are now numerous studies from nearly all parts of the world, documenting the severe long-term impacts of trawling. The damage exceeds over half of the seabed area of many fishing grounds, and worse in inner and middle parts of the continental shelves with particular damage to small-scale coastal fishing communities. Indeed, while very light trawling may be sustainable or even increase abundance and productivity of a few taxa, new studies, including data from over a century ago, clearly indicate damage to the seabed across large portions of the fishing grounds and, at worst, reductions in pristine taxa of 20–80% including both demersals and benthic fauna. Unlike their shallow-water counterparts, deep-sea communities recover slowly, over decades and centuries, from such impacts. Some might not recover at all if faced with additional pressures including climate change and might lead to a permanent reduction in the productivity of fishing grounds. There are now discussions ongoing within several bodies including the FAO [Food and Agriculture Organization of the United Nations] on developing better international guidelines for the management of deep-sea fisheries in the high seas, but substantial action is urgently needed given the cumulative threats that the oceans are facing.

Primary fishing grounds are likely to become increasingly infested by invasive species, many introduced from ship ballast water.

The vulnerability of impacted ecosystems to additional stresses is also demonstrated by the increase of invasive species infestations that are concentrated in the same 10–15% of the world's oceans. Heavily disturbed and damaged marine areas are more likely to have a higher vulnerability to infestations brought in by ships plying the world's oceans despite recommendations in many areas for mid-ocean exchange of ballast water. Geographical distribution of invasive species suggests a strong relationship between their occurrence and disturbed, polluted and overfished areas and in particular the location of major shipping routes at a global scale. It appears that the most devastating outbreaks of such marine infestations have been brought in along the major shipping routes and primarily established in the most intensively fished and polluted areas on the continental shelves. Growing climate change will most likely accelerate these invasions further.

Climate Change's Devastating Impact

The worst concentration of cumulative impacts of climate change with existing pressures of overharvest, bottom trawling, invasive species, coastal development and pollution appear to be concentrated in 10–15% of the oceans concurrent with today's most important fishing grounds.

Climate change, with its potential effects on ocean thermohaline circulation and a potential future decline in natural 'flushing and cleaning' mechanisms, shifts in the distributions of marine life, coral bleaching, acidification and stressed ecosystems will compound the impacts of other stressors like overharvest, bottom trawling, coastal pollution and introduced species. The combined actions of climate change and other human pressures will increase the vulnerability of the world's most productive fishing grounds—with serious ecological, economic and social implications. The potential effects are likely to be most pronounced for developing countries where fish are an increasingly important and valuable export product, and there is limited scope for mitigation or adaptation.

A lack of good marine data, poor funding for ocean observations and an 'out of sight—out of mind' mentality may have led to greater environmental degradation in the sea than would have been allowed on land.

A substantially increased focus must be devoted to building and strengthening the resilience of marine ecosystems.

The lack of marine information and easy observation by humans as land-living organisms, along with insufficient funds for monitoring, may result in these and other pressures to progress further than anything we have yet seen or would have permitted without intervention on land, even though the oceans represent a significant share of global economies and basic food supply. Lack of good governance, particularly of the high seas, but also in many exclusive economic zones (EEZs) where the primary focus is economic gain, has resulted in limited flexibility or incentive to shift to ecosystem-based management. The potential for climate change to disrupt natural cycles in ocean productivity adds to the urgency to better manage our oceans. The loss and impoverishment of these highly diverse marine ecosystems on Earth and modification of the marine food chain will have profound effects on life in the seas and human well-being in the future.

Substantial resources need to be allocated to reducing climate and non-climate pressures. Priority needs to be given to protecting substantial areas of the continental shelves. These initiatives are required to build resilience against climate change and to ensure that further collapses in fish stocks are avoided in coming decades.

Urgent efforts to control accelerating climate change are needed, but this alone will not be sufficient. A substantially increased focus must be devoted to building and strengthening the resilience of marine ecosystems. Synergistic threats and impacts need to be addressed in a synergistic way, via application of an ecosystem and integrated ocean management approach. Actions for a reduction of coastal pollution, establishment of marine protected areas in deeper waters, protection of seamounts and parts (likely at least 20%) of the continental shelves against bottom trawling and other extractive activity, and stronger regulation of fisheries all have to go hand in hand. Unless these actions are taken immediately, the resilience of most fishing grounds in the world, and their ability to recover, will further diminish. Accelerating climate change and inaction risks an unprecedented, dramatic and widespread collapse of marine ecosystems and fisheries within the next decades.

Brazil's Ethanol Production Is Not Contributing to the Global Food Shortage

Maggie Airriess

In the following viewpoint, Maggie Airriess, research associate at the Council on Hemispheric Affairs, argues that the Brazilian government's approach to ethanol production is good for the environment and the world food supply. She sharply criticizes the U.S. government's overproduction of ethanol and recent import/ export policies, which have contributed to the global food shortage. In addition to increased efficiency in production, Brazil has improved its actions to increase environmental conservation and small agricultural efforts.

As you read, consider the following questions:

1. What is the current U.S. tariff on sugar-based ethanol?
2. By what percentage has agricultural aid to poor countries dropped from 1980 to 2005?
3. How much ethanol does Brazil produce annually?

U.S.-Brazil tension, a relatively recent development, resurfaced during the UN [United Nations] World Food Summit in Rome on June 3–5 [2008], encouraging the booming Brazilian sugar-based ethanol market to increase its new de-

Maggie Airriess, "Don't Blame Brazil for the World's Food Crisis!" *Brazzil Magazine*, July 15, 2008. Reproduced by permission.

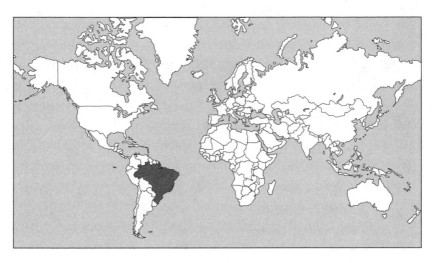

velopment projects. This rift represents a de facto counter-move against the far less efficient U.S. model predicated on corn-based ethanol production.

Following the summit, Brazilian officials began a weeklong tour, stopping in Morocco, Algeria and Tunisia, during which they discussed a set of commercial agreements that will boost multilateral cooperation with several African countries. The trade agreements, projected to begin in 2009, include an expansion in ethanol investment, urbanism, air and sea transport, and cooperation in professional training between the two regions.

In a statement that appeared in *Brazzil* magazine, Brazilian Secretary of Development Ivan Ramalho remarked that he hoped the meetings would enhance trade with other countries in order to diminish Brazil's overreliance on the U.S. market. Brazil's recent trade initiatives with other developing countries have emerged largely due to the reluctance of some developed nations to lower trade subsidies. This impedes Brazil's ability to trade, adding significantly to the current debate over rising food prices.

In an official statement released after the first set of meetings, Michel Alaby, secretary general of the Arab Brazilian

Chamber of Commerce, called for solidarity among countries suffering from rising food prices and demanded that developed countries, especially the U.S. and Europe, eliminate international trade barriers in the agricultural sector.

With the emerging agreements, Brazilian officials hope to call attention to the U.S.'s highly inefficient corn-based ethanol production at the height of a snowballing food crisis. The government aspires to be a strong actor in the midst of the food crisis and plans to show the rest of the world the benefits of Brazil's efficient sugar ethanol market, while it professes to be executing projects stalling the destruction of the Amazon rain forest.

U.S. Subsidies and World Hunger

On June 16, following petitions from the Brazilian government, the World Trade Organization (WTO) condemned the U.S. for its agricultural subsidies that unfairly favor domestic producers. The WTO largely blamed Washington's practices for the world food crisis that may leave an additional 100 million people hungry by the end of 2008.

The WTO criticized U.S. actions as "an attempt to disrespect international commercial regulation with subsidies that drastically reduced domestic prices and could have been seriously damaging for developing nations like Brazil."

During the [World] Food Summit, which was hosted by the UN Food and Agriculture Organization (FAO), U.S. representatives argued in favor of their protectionist policies, claiming that biofuels are environmentally safer than petroleum, and also benefit farmers, entrepreneurs, and consumers.

Under pressure from formidable agricultural lobby groups, the U.S. Congress recently placed a 54-cent per gallon tariff on sugar-based ethanol, hoping to encourage domestic ethanol production. As result of the tariff, U.S. ethanol production increased and Brazilian ethanol exports fell significantly in 2007. Efforts to remove the tariffs have faced strong resistance from both corn and sugar lobbyists, impeding any kind of remedial actions on surging grain prices.

As economist C. Ford Runge, a commodity and trade specialist at the Center for International Food and Agricultural Policy, confirms, "If you want to take some of the pressure off the U.S. market, the obvious thing to do is lower that tariff and let some Brazilian ethanol come in." Supporters of this policy believe that increasing Brazilian ethanol production would push down overall energy costs.

The average French cow receives more financial support than half of the world's population earns daily.

Increasing Assistance to Developing Countries

Since the summit, the UN has called on the international community to increase its assistance to developing countries severely affected by the current food crisis. UN officials have planned visits to several African countries to discuss possible food security solutions. In addition, the FAO published several reports criticizing the U.S. and Europe for unnecessarily subsidizing crops and inadvertently driving up food prices while shifting food production in less-developed countries where small farmers cannot effectively compete.

The *Guardian* noted from the reports that the U.S. government is currently spending US$7 billion annually on subsidies, while the European Union spends around 43 billion euros (US$67.5 billion). A striking example can be seen in France, where the average French cow receives more financial support than half the world's population earns daily.

With rich countries dominating global trade that greatly affects ethanol, FAO Director-General Jacques Diouf says that funding for agricultural programs in developing countries increasingly suffers with agricultural aid to poor countries having dropped 56% from 1980 to 2005. "Now more than ever private decisions being made about food production into ethanol are affecting all parts of the globe, with little response from the leaders that could do the most," Diouf observed.

One main concern over how biofuel policy disrupts the market is the current excessive power that interest groups have in the debate on subsidies in developed nations. Instead of catering to special interests, U.S. politicians would be well advised to cooperate with other countries. While the UN works diligently to halt the growing food shortage, world leaders refuse to amend restrictions on food exports. This negligence is inexcusable on both economic and humanitarian grounds.

Not All Ethanol Is the Same

In defense of sugar-based ethanol, [Brazilian] President [Luiz Inácio] Lula [da Silva] stated that the U.S. misguidedly produces corn for ethanol instead of other agricultural products, while keeping subsidies high to benefit U.S. multinational companies. [President] Lula argues that this is another case where the U.S. keeps developing countries from playing an influential role in the world economy.

He claimed, "I am sorry to see that many of those who blame ethanol, including from sugarcane, for the high price of food are the same ones who for decades have maintained protectionist policies to the detriment of farmers in poor countries and of consumers in the entire world."

The U.S. misguidedly produces corn for ethanol instead of other agricultural products.

In comparison with corn-based ethanol, sugar-based ethanol is more efficient, cheaper to produce, and uses less valuable land. According to the World Bank's *Biofuels: The Promise and the Risks*, the U.S. ethanol industry currently uses 10 million hectares, while Brazil only uses 3.6 million of such terrain and produces eight to ten times more energy than that produced from corn.

Brazil does not subsidize sugar, which helps sustain global sugar prices. Whereas corn prices have surged 65% in the last five years, which many argue is the result of U.S. subsidies. Brazilian ethanol also yields 8.3 times more energy than the fossil fuels used to produce it, while corn ethanol yields only 1.5 times the energy it consumes.

Further ethanol controversy surrounds environmentalist concerns that Brazil's sugar industry is permanently destroying large areas of the Amazon rain forest. The industry has forced small farmers to sell their land at low prices and work for large multinational companies, under poor conditions and scant pay. In addition, Brazil's ethanol production has pushed soybean cultivation and cattle ranching into the Amazon area, making room for sugarcane production in the southeastern part of the country.

In comparison with corn-based ethanol, sugar-based ethanol is more efficient, cheaper to produce, and uses less valuable land.

This region, once home to coffee and fruit plantations, was originally part of the southeastern portion of the Amazon rain forest, of which only 7% remains today. Another environmental concern regarding sugarcane cultivation involves the burning of the old cane to get rid of dry leaves and dispensable biomass. This hazardous practice creates health problems for local populations, and spreads the fires into some of the remaining Amazon rain forests.

Increasing Environmental Concerns

President Lula has increasingly displayed support to protect the Amazon from ongoing destruction. On June 19, the gov-

"Oil vs. Food," cartoon by Khalil Bendib, March 10, 2008. © www.bendib.com. All rights reserved.

ernment extended its two-year ban on the sale of soy from the deforested land in Amazonia until July 2009. Additionally, officials from the Brazilian Institute of Environment and Renewable Natural Resources have already begun bans on beef and timber from illegal Amazon lands.

This recent commitment could signify the government's sincerity regarding prevention of deforestation and "its commitment to a policy of environmental registration and licensing for land in Amazonia."

The Lula administration is taking urgent steps to enhance agricultural production and increase Amazonian protection.

New policies also present Brazil as environmentally conscious to international groups such as Greenpeace, who have in the past heavily criticized the country's lack of effort in sustaining the Amazon's integrity.

Greenpeace director Paulo Adario applauded Lula, stating, "Today's decision is important because it proves that it's possible to guarantee food production without cutting down one more hectare of Amazon forest." Also, in an attempt to speed the recovery of Amazonian pastures and degraded soils, the government will offer soft loans, ample credit for small farmers, and an insurance system designed to reduce the risks of climate change.

With the appointment of strong conservationists such as the Minister of Environment, Carlos Minc, a UN awarded defender of the environment, the Lula administration is taking urgent steps to enhance agricultural production and increase Amazonian protection. If action indeed follows such rhetoric, Brazilian planners could be on the verge of helping the country become a world player in trade while it attempts to keep domestic prices low.

Currently, Brazil produces 5.8 billion gallons of ethanol annually, but exports only 960 million gallons. Yet the energy giant is capable of providing the world with 52 billion gallons a year if, through new foreign investment, the government can put in an additional US$9.5 billion for financing pipelines, terminals and new plants, offsetting the international dependence on OPEC [Organization of the Petroleum Exporting Countries].

As ethanol increasingly becomes a fixture in the global energy debate, these new steps could mark significant progress in fighting the global food crisis, while drawing increasing international scrutiny to the irresponsible, self-interested subsidy initiatives stealthily exhibited by the U.S., Europe, and Japan.

The Kenyan Food Shortage Threatens the Health of HIV Sufferers

IRIN

In the following viewpoint, IRIN argues that the severe food shortage in Kenya is taking its toll on HIV/AIDS sufferers. Lack of food reduces their ability to take life-saving antiretroviral (ARV) drugs, which cause nausea, weakness, and dizziness if taken on an empty stomach. Additional complications of the food shortage include hungry individuals resorting to prostitution and other means of feeding their families. Support groups for Kenyans stricken with HIV/AIDS are less effective, given that few members have the money to pay for transportation to meetings. IRIN is a humanitarian news and analysis service that is part of the United Nations Office for the Coordination of Humanitarian Affairs.

As you read, consider the following questions:

1. According to IRIN, what is considered a healthy BMI?
2. What are three main causes of the food crisis in Kenya, as described in the viewpoint?
3. As stated in the viewpoint, what percentage of people in Makueni, Kenya, have HIV?

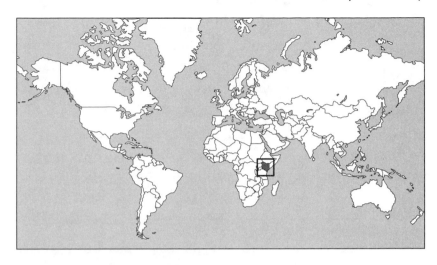

Makueni District Hospital in eastern Kenya has recorded a significant drop in the weight of several of its HIV-positive patients . . . , which nutritionists ascribe to severe food shortages across much of the country.

"We have a large number of patients with a BMI [body mass index, a measure of nutritional status] below the healthy cutoff of 18.5," Fransiscah Yula, a nutritionist at the hospital, told IRIN/PlusNews.

An estimated 10 million Kenyans are battling a food crisis as a result of crop failure due to poor rains and drought, high food prices, and the effects of postelection violence in early 2008 that disrupted farming activities in Rift Valley Province, the country's breadbasket.

Yula said she counselled HIV-positive patients to eat a healthy, balanced diet, but the advice was somewhat ironic under the circumstances. "Most of the patients we see tell us they have one meal per day; some take drugs on empty stomachs," she said.

"It would help if the distribution of relief food was accompanied by the distribution of nutritious complements like tinned meat, vegetables and fruit to help provide these people with a nutritional balance—the food they eat at home is not nutrient-dense at all."

Poor nutrition weakens the body's defences against the virus, hastens progress from HIV to AIDS, and makes it difficult to take antiretroviral (ARV) drugs, which can increase appetite. Enough food can help reduce some side effects of ARVs and promote adherence to drug regimens.

Enough food can help reduce some side effects of [antiretroviral drugs] and promote adherence to drug regimens.

The food shortages in Makueni are evidenced by farmland lying fallow, long queues of people patiently waiting for maize-meal donations at a local political party's headquarters, and riverbeds so dry that people have to dig a hole to find water.

Health workers say local residents have begun to resort to dangerous practices to put food on the table. "In December we got reports that men were sending their wives out to sleep with other men in exchange for food," said Albanus Mutiso, the district HIV/AIDS and sexually transmitted infections coordinator for Makueni district. "You know the situation is desperate if people are going to that extent to find food."

He said rations for HIV-positive people were often insufficient because they were intended for one person but were used to feed entire families. "A mother will almost always feed her children before herself, so she remains undernourished," he noted. "Recently we saw a pregnant HIV-positive woman who weighed just 35 kilos [about 77 pounds]—unless the government moves in swiftly, people will die."

Makueni has an HIV prevalence of 7 percent in a population of about 290,000, slightly lower than the national prevalence of 7.4 percent; 73 percent of the people live below the poverty line, and just 26 percent earn a wage, leaving the rest to depend mainly on subsistence farming to make a living.

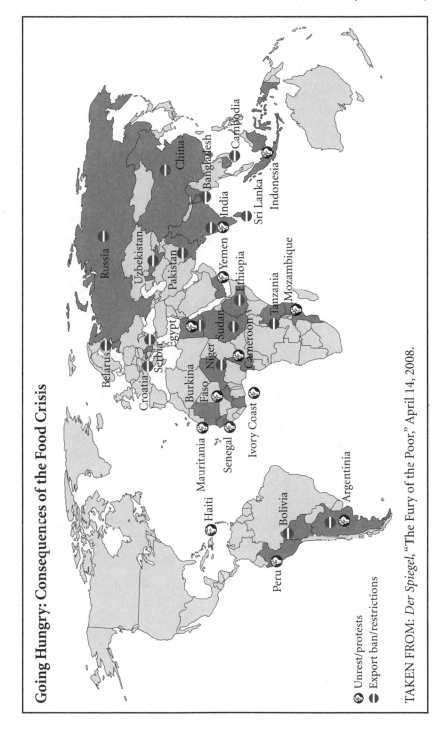

Going Hungry: Consequences of the Food Crisis

Unrest/protests

Export ban/restrictions

TAKEN FROM: *Der Spiegel*, "The Fury of the Poor," April 14, 2008.

Harder to Adhere

"I weigh 48 kilos [about 106 pounds] now—I sometimes go one month without drinking milk and three months without eating meat," said Mbula Waema, an HIV-positive widow who is caring for a family of ten.

Her obvious malnutrition deeply concerns Millicent Ondigo, who coordinates Zingatia Maisha, an HIV drug-adherence support programme run by the African Medical and Research Foundation (AMREF), which has its headquarters in Nairobi, the Kenyan capital. "I have never seen Mbula like this; I'm very worried about what would happen if she got sick now."

Rations for HIV-positive people were often insufficient because they were intended for one person but were used to feed entire families.

Despite the fact that Waema eats one meal a day—usually a cup of porridge—she has continued to take her life-prolonging ARV medication because she knows that interrupting her regimen could mean death, but taking the drugs on an empty stomach is hard.

"I feel weak, nauseous and dizzy—my stomach burns when I don't eat well and take the medicine," she said. "It's difficult to farm when I'm this weak, but I have to. . . . When I feel too dizzy I sit under a tree and rest." Waema farms sisal plants, from which she weaves ropes for sale in the local market, otherwise her family will starve.

Marietta Nzula, 38, is more fortunate; she lives at her family's homestead near the town of Kathonzweni in Makueni. "My family makes sure I get treatment when I'm sick, and even now, when times are tough, at least I get some of the children's uji [porridge] so I can have something in my stomach to take my medication," she said. "My brother's wife reminds me to take my drugs every morning—they are very good to me."

Nzula says she wishes she was able to do her part to keep the family afloat; she feels that especially in hard times such as these, she is a burden her family could do without.

Support Networks Under Pressure

Although the traditional community support systems still exist, they are stretched to breaking point said Onesmus Mutungi, who heads two local HIV support groups.

"I eat two or three meals a day, which makes me better off than most, so I share with those who have less," he told IRIN/PlusNews. "But now, even in my home, things are tight, and sharing my food means that I eat less, so I feel weak when I take my medication."

Mutungi said it was getting harder to persuade support group members to stay on their medication when they did not have enough food. "None of them have stopped taking their ARVs, but many are tempted to do so," he said.

President Mwai Kibaki has declared Kenya's food crisis a national disaster.

"We can't hold additional support meetings because transport costs are too high—many people aren't even coming to the meetings because they can't afford the matatu [minibus-taxi] fare."

AMREF's Ondigo said Zingatia Maisha was working with local NGOs [nongovernmental organizations] and the government to try to provide the HIV support groups with food supplements so they would be less likely to interrupt their treatment regimens.

Food

President Mwai Kibaki has declared Kenya's food crisis a national disaster and the government has appealed for 37 billion Kenya shillings (US$400 million) to meet the needs of the food-insecure.

Asia Faces a Food Shortage by 2050 Without Water Reform

International Water Management Institute

The International Water Management Institute (IWMI) is a nonprofit organization spanning ten countries in Asia and Africa that seeks to improve the management of land and water resources. In the following viewpoint, the group argues that if Asia does not radically improve its irrigation system, the region may face widespread food shortages by 2050. Given that Asian agriculture depends heavily upon irrigation, continuing to rely on systems that are more than thirty years old could lead to large-scale crop failure. IWMI recommends updating the irrigation systems and teaching farmers sustainable farming methods.

As you read, consider the following questions:

1. According to expert estimates, by how much will the demand for food and animal feed crops in Asia increase in the next fifty years?

2. What are some problems of past irrigation systems in Asia, as stated in the viewpoint?

3. On average how long have most irrigation systems in Asia been operating?

International Water Management Institute, *Asia's Irrigation: To Sustainably Meet Tomorrow's Food Needs*, Colombo, Sri Lanka: International Water Management Institute, 2009. Copyright © 2009 International Water Management Institute. Reproduced by permission.

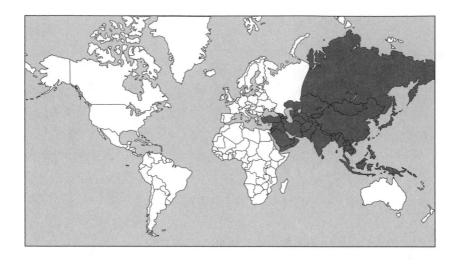

Ending hunger, given Asia's swelling population, increasing urbanization and climate change, presents a huge challenge for farmers. With land and water resources stretched, they must double their output from existing cultivated areas. Irrigation systems will be vital to help meet future food needs and reverse past environmental degradation, even given higher yields from rainfed agriculture. However, the irrigation sector must first be revitalized to unlock its potential, by introducing innovative practices and changing the way it is governed and managed.

Irrigation developments are often instrumental in achieving high rates of agricultural growth.

Why Is Irrigation Important in Asia?

Asia contains 70% of the world's irrigated area ...

Irrigated agriculture has been at the heart of rural growth in Asia. Here, 34% of cultivated land is irrigated, as compared to only 10% in North America and 6% in Africa.

... and irrigation was key to the success of the Green Revolution ...

Despite forecasts of famine and starvation, most Asian countries became food self-sufficient in the 1970s and 1980s, thanks to the Green Revolution. Timely and reliable water supplies, greater cropping intensities, high-yielding varieties of seeds and doses of fertilizers pushed up productivity.

. . . this helped alleviate poverty and boost rural growth.

In South Asia, cereal production rose by 137% from 1970 to 2007 with only a 3% increase in the amount of land used. In East and Southeast Asia, agricultural productivities more than tripled and rural poverty declined rapidly. Studies show that, depending on the stage of development, agricultural growth is often more effective at alleviating poverty than growth in other sectors. Irrigation developments are often instrumental in achieving high rates of agricultural growth.

Does Asia Still Need to Invest in Irrigation?

Asia needs to feed a growing population . . .

Feeding the extra 1.5 billion people who will live on the continent by 2050 will require more food than the region currently produces. Experts estimate that demand for food and animal feed crops will double during the next 50 years. Growing this extra food will require better management of existing irrigated lands, since opening up new frontiers is constrained by lack of land and water resources.

Some 700 million Asians, mostly concentrated in South Asia, live on less than US$1 per day.

. . . secure livelihoods and alleviate poverty . . .

In spite of progress made in recent decades some 700 million Asians, mostly concentrated in South Asia, live on less than US$1 per day. The Asian Development Bank (ADB) estimates that roughly half of Asia's population will still be rural in 2030. Therefore, farming will continue to provide livelihoods and food security for many people.

... within the limits of natural resources ...

There is very little scope for expanding arable land in most regions of Asia, so developing extensive new irrigation schemes is not a solution. Similarly, there are clear limits in most places on the amount of additional water that can be used for agriculture.

... while limiting stress to the environment.

The need to produce more food is prompting renewed interest in Asia's irrigation. However, this must be done in a way that conserves the vital environmental services that wetlands, rivers and other ecosystems provide.

Boosting the performance of irrigated agriculture will be critical.

Investments to raise yields and productivity from irrigated land must be key elements of a strategy to produce the extra food needed, while safeguarding the environment from additional stresses. Alternative options, such as upgrading rainfed farming and increasing international trade in food grains, must also contribute, but they will need to be supplemented by a significant increase in production from irrigated agriculture.

The need to produce more food is prompting renewed interest in Asia's irrigation.

Will Past Irrigation Schemes Be Effective in the Future?

Irrigation was key to raising productivity 50 years ago ...

Irrigation, from large-scale surface schemes and private groundwater supplies, played an important role in raising productivity during the Green Revolution. The increase in food production outpaced population growth and helped alleviate poverty.

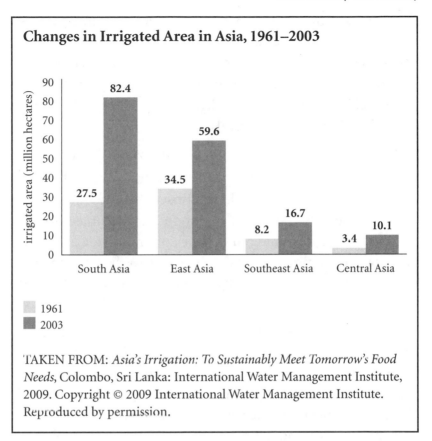

Changes in Irrigated Area in Asia, 1961–2003

TAKEN FROM: *Asia's Irrigation: To Sustainably Meet Tomorrow's Food Needs*, Colombo, Sri Lanka: International Water Management Institute, 2009. Copyright © 2009 International Water Management Institute. Reproduced by permission.

... but the face of Asia is changing fast.

Asia is now a very different place to what it was in the 1960s and 1970s. Rural people have more opportunities to work outside agriculture, and increasing urbanization has boosted wealth for many.

Producing food for a meat- or milk-based diet requires more water than for a vegetarian one.

Wealthier city dwellers have new dietary demands...

Wealth influences dietary choices and diets affect water use. Providing the foods that people now demand requires shifts in agriculture. In many places, such as China, the demand for meat is increasing. Producing food for a meat- or milk-based diet requires more water than for a vegetarian one. Meanwhile, growing a range of crops requires a different irrigation regime than that needed to supply water to large areas planted with one or two cereals.

. . . which are providing farmers with opportunities.

The shift from rural to urban living has provided farmers with more options. Some have chosen to quit farming for city-based jobs, while others have opted to become part-time farmers. Those remaining in the agricultural sector have taken advantage of improved access to markets to diversify their activities and produce the higher-value niche crops urban residents demand.

Meanwhile, state-built irrigation schemes are underperforming . . .

The large-scale, centrally managed irrigation schemes of the past were not designed to be demand driven or provide the reliable, flexible and equitable year-round water service that modern farming methods require. Beset with problems of inappropriate design, poor maintenance, salinity and waterlogging, many large-scale schemes are currently in decline across Asia. Efforts by many national governments to rehabilitate them are ongoing but the results are, at best, mixed.

. . . forcing farmers to invest on their own.

With poor service provisions and a lack of effective management, farmers have taken irrigation into their own hands by pumping water from aquifers, rivers and drains. Privately sourced, pumped groundwater now represents the bulk of irrigation in large parts of South, East and Southeast Asia. Many farmers are investing in on-farm storage ponds to augment their supply and gain greater control over their water supplies.

What Is the Best Way Forward for Asian Irrigation?

Irrigated agriculture still offers huge opportunities ...

There is considerable scope to increase food production, enhance livelihoods and reduce poverty in existing irrigated areas. However, realizing this potential will require new approaches to investing in infrastructure, reforming institutions and building capacity.

... but only innovative strategies will unlock the potential gains.

Future irrigation systems will need to be efficient and flexible to meet the demands of many sectors including farming, fishing, domestic use and energy supply. The managers of irrigation systems will need to find ways to generate more value from ecosystem services and halt environmental degradation. They must also enable farmers to respond to challenges posed by volatile market conditions and climate change.

Tomorrow's managers will need to look beyond the confines of the irrigation system and start managing operations within entire river basins.

Recommended Strategies

Strategy 1: Modernize yesteryear's schemes for tomorrow's needs. In Asia, most irrigation schemes have operated for 30 to 40 years. Surface irrigation schemes across Asia have become underused, poorly maintained and inefficient. Many would benefit from being modernized, by being redesigned, operated and managed for a range of uses. For example, surface irrigation schemes could be used to recharge aquifers or fill intermediate storage structures, such as farm ponds, providing farmers with greater reliability and control. Meanwhile, flexible and responsive management will be vital for mitigating against, and adapting to, climate change. Tomorrow's managers will need to look beyond the confines of the irrigation system and start managing operations within entire river basins. This will involve allocating water to multiple uses and to meet environmental targets.

Strategy 2: Go with the flow by supporting farmers' initiatives. While the area of surface irrigation has remained stagnant or has been shrinking, farmers in South, East and Southeast Asia have raised yields using locally adapted irrigation technologies to scavenge water from surface sources, wastewater and groundwater. There are opportunities for investors to identify successful initiatives and direct funds towards schemes emulating farmers' methods. New models are needed for managing groundwater in areas where this pump-based 'atomistic' irrigation has largely replaced centralized surface irrigation.

Strategy 3: Look beyond conventional PIM/IMT [participatory irrigation management/irrigation management transfer] recipes. Efforts to reform large-scale irrigation schemes by transferring management to farmers have had less-than-expected success throughout Asia. Many believe the private sector could help irrigation entities improve water delivery. For example, irrigation departments could outsource irrigation services, create public-private partnerships or provide incentives for irrigation officials to act as entrepreneurs in publicly managed operations. Such actions could help to mobilize funds, increase efficiency and improve the provision of water services but are, as yet, rare and largely untested.

Strategy 4: Expand capacity and knowledge. If new approaches are to be successful, investors will need to direct funds towards training existing staff, attracting new talent through forward-thinking curricula and realistic remuneration packages, as well as building the capacity of all stakeholders (including the irrigation bureaucracy). Initiatives might include updating engineering courses in universities, conducting in-depth training workshops for farmers and irrigation officials, or revamping irrigation departments to empower their workforces.

Strategy 5: Invest outside the irrigation sector. The irrigation sector is embedded within Asia's wider political economy and is, therefore, affected by external forces. Policies and programs that influence agriculture, both directly and indirectly, come to drive developments in irrigation. Framing policies to ensure external influences on the water sector are properly understood and planned is one way to indirectly influence irrigation performance.

Ukraine Can Prevent a Worldwide Food Shortage

Jim Davis

In the following viewpoint, Jim Davis, a regular contributor to Ukraine Business News, *argues that Ukraine could contribute greatly to global food needs if its governing leaders and farming industry executives prepare for the opportunity. Overcoming drought conditions, disease infestations, and grain storage problems will not be easy to accomplish, but Davis asserts that selective investments and improvements in communication will put Ukraine on the right path to growing the grains needed to feed the world's hungry.*

As you read, consider the following questions:

1. As explained by Davis, what is the expected world population total for the middle of this century?
2. What is Ug99?
3. By what percentage did world food prices rise in 2007, as cited in the viewpoint?

A combination of both natural and manmade events around the world has coincided to bring grains, particularly wheat, to some of the highest prices since wheat futures trading began. This price escalation has occurred at a time when world food supplies are as insecure [as] they have been in decades.

Jim Davis, "Ukraine's Role in Increasing World Food Security," *Unian*, February 4, 2008. Reproduced by permission of the author.

The UN's Food and Agriculture Organization (FAO), head-quartered in Rome, believes that Ukraine is uniquely positioned to make a major impact on meeting world food needs, but many wonder if Ukraine has the political will to take advantage of the opportunities the new demands and explosive market conditions present

Bloomberg reports that the most-active contract more than doubled in the past year and reached a record USD [U.S. dollars] 13.495 per bushel on Feb. 27 [2007], based on speculation that farmers would not produce enough to meet global demand. Futures fell back from the highs but have now begun a new upward march with no discernible end in sight.

Wheat on the Chicago Board of Trade, generally the reference point for grain traders worldwide, rose by the exchange-imposed maximum of 90 cents on March 13 to trade above USD 13 a bushel for the first time since the February 27 record setter. The price gained 16% in three days, March 11–13, the biggest such gain in weeks.

Unprecedented Grain Drain

Jim Asher, a Kansas-native agricultural expert who has been involved in Ukrainian agriculture since 1993, said he could remember only a few times in his 70 years involved with farming that futures had been higher.

Asher also pointed out that the current situation in which wheat and soybean futures are almost equal in price is, as far as he knows, unprecedented. "Wheat futures are usually only about half the price of soy futures," Asher said, adding that the high prices have already made farming in Ukraine more profitable with more upside potential.

The United States' wheat stockpiles will probably drop by May 31 [2008] to 242 million bushels, down 47% from 456 million a year earlier, the U.S. Department of Agriculture [USDA] said on March 11. USDA also said that global stockpiles are expected to fall 12% from a year earlier to 110.4 million tonnes by May 31, the lowest since 1978.

Australia is normally a major exporter of grain, usually second only to the United States. In a good year, Australia would hope to harvest about 25 million tonnes. However, some of Australia's most productive grain areas have suffered years of drought, believed to be related to changing world climate patterns. The Land Down Under saw its 2006 crop yield only 9.8 million tonnes.

The Australian drought is one of the major reasons for the low level of global wheat stocks. Visiting Nottingham, a small agriculture community in rural New South Wales, home to a massive grain storage complex, a BBC reporter described a usually overflowing silo the size of a medieval cathedral as being so empty it felt like a giant echo chamber.

The increasing number of mouths to feed puts pressure on a wide range of resources.

More Mouths to Feed

Some consistent rains in critical areas, assuming that they come, could solve many of the problems caused by the great

Australian drought, but even that would leave grain demand—and prices—high because of other factors that are much longer term in their effects.

The first and perhaps most important reason is growth in the world's population, now expected to rise above nine billion by about the middle of this century. The increasing number of mouths to feed puts pressure on a wide range of resources, including land, water and petroleum, as well as the food supply.

However, much of the overall population growth is in areas where the economies are booming, particularly China and India, increasing its impact. When you combine the two population giants, you have accounted for almost three billion or about a third of the humans alive today.

For many of the increasing numbers of Chinese and Indian citizens, their newfound wealth allows them to be active consumers, and that usually manifests itself first in movement from a subsistence diet to a more meat-intensive diet. Moreover, the prosperity-driven demand for more meat increases the demand for more grain for livestock production.

New Diseases Add to World's Food Woes

A little-known wheat disease is now beginning to spread into parts of the world where it could do immense harm. The killer fungus, called Ug99, is a virulent strain of black stem rust (*Puccinia graminis*). Scientists report that most of the wheat grown in Africa, Asia and China has little resistance to Ug99.

First identified in Uganda in 1999, Ug99 has since invaded Kenya and Ethiopia and, last year, Yemen. Based on earlier fungal invasions, scientists had expected prevailing winds to carry Ug99 spores to Egypt, Turkey and Syria, and only later to Iran, a major wheat grower, giving Iran some time to prepare for the problems that Ug99 brings.

However, with Cyclone Gonu hitting the Arabian peninsula in June 2007, the fungus reached Iran one to two years earlier than expected.

Researchers now fear that the winds could also have blown the fungus spores into Pakistan, which lies north of Yemen, and unfortunately, where it has become difficult to keep track of its spread because of the war in neighbouring Afghanistan. What makes the situation worse is that Ug99 is now resistant to the three major antirust genes used in nearly all the world's wheat.

Though scientists hope to slow the fungus's spread by spraying fungicide or even stopping farmers from planting wheat in the spores' path, the only real remedy remains new wheat varieties that resist Ug99. However, researchers warn that these may not be ready for five years.

High prices for corn ... have led to the conversion of hundreds of thousands of hectares of former wheat lands.

The SUV Factor

Expanded populations and booming economies in India and China explain part of the current grain imbalance, but at least as great an impact comes from the massive expansion, particularly in the United States, of the use of biofuels, particularly ethanol.

High prices for corn, the preferred feedstock for ethanol production, have led to the conversion of hundreds of thousands of hectares of former wheat lands to corn and sorghum for ethanol and rape and soy for biodiesel.

So long as the United States federal government and many state governments in rural states provide subsidies for biofuel production, it is likely that farmers will continue their conversion of former wheat lands to those grain and oilseed plantings they see as adding to their profit potential.

The administration of U.S. President George W. Bush [2008] has been very reluctant to implement widespread demands for more fuel-efficient vehicle standards.

This failure of the U.S. government to exert leadership in energy conservation and America's love affair with behemoth sport-utility vehicles [SUVs] has led to continued increases in fuel consumption, in spite of the highest gasoline prices in U.S. history.

Unless the next administration, which begins in January 2009, makes much stronger efforts in this sector, the United States is likely to remain the world's most profligate user of petroleum.

Moreover, the expanded use of biofuels, particularly ethanol, in the United States has led to hundreds of thousands of hectares of land formerly used for food grain production being converted to the production of corn for ethanol production.

Futures prices as far ahead as two years are so high as to suggest that the market considers higher corn prices to become a permanent fixture, thus fueling the rationale for raising corn.

The expanded use of biofuels ... has led to hundreds of thousands of hectares of land formerly used for food grain production being converted to the production of corn for ethanol production.

Feeding the Poor

According to the FAO, world food prices rose by almost 40% in 2007. Without action to counteract some of the issues described above, the food price spiral could continue and even become worse. This presents a problem not only to average citizens, but also increases the costs of providing food aid to war-torn and drought-stricken areas of Africa and Asia.

Further, those countries with large populations of urban poor tend to subsidise food supplies, particularly for basics such as bread. The current situation will create increase problems for those countries and may even result in regime changes in some.

The European Bank for Reconstruction and Development (EBRD) and the FAO organised a conference in London on March 10, 2008, to explore options to foster better cooperation between the private and public sectors in dealing with the problems.

Senior government officials from Eastern Europe and the former Soviet Union met with executives from the private agribusiness sector to seek concrete proposals to boost agricultural investments and unlock unused output potential.

The conference's aim was to emphasise that it is crucial to increase investments not only in primary agriculture but also in the whole range of agricultural infrastructure and the processing industry.

Ukraine is probably the only one ... that ... could supply the 50 million additional tones of wheat needed to fill the grain bins of the world.

One of Ukraine's best-known and most highly respected agricultural experts, Leonid Kozachenko, a former vice prime minister for the agricultural sector and currently head of the Ukrainian Agrarian Confederation (UAC), was a featured participant at the London conference.

He said that the FAO believes that only four countries in the world have significant untapped capacity to make a major impact on the growing food security needs—Ukraine, Russia, Kazakhstan and Argentina.

He added that Ukraine is probably the only one of the four that, properly organised and motivated, could supply the 50 million additional tonnes of wheat needed to fill the grain

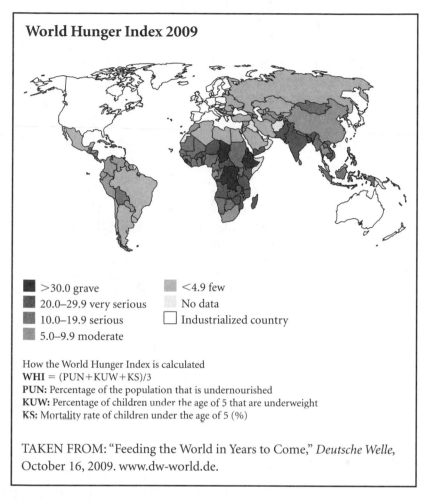

World Hunger Index 2009

- ■ >30.0 grave
- ■ 20.0–29.9 very serious
- ■ 10.0–19.9 serious
- ■ 5.0–9.9 moderate
- ■ <4.9 few
- No data
- ☐ Industrialized country

How the World Hunger Index is calculated
WHI = (PUN+KUW+KS)/3
PUN: Percentage of the population that is undernourished
KUW: Percentage of children under the age of 5 that are underweight
KS: Mortality rate of children under the age of 5 (%)

TAKEN FROM: "Feeding the World in Years to Come," *Deutsche Welle*,
October 16, 2009. www.dw-world.de.

bins of the world sufficiently to alleviate the gaps caused by expanded food demand, weather problems and the food-to-biofuel conversion of agricultural land.

Reversing Negative Trends

Both EBRD and FAO believe that there is significant untapped agricultural production potential in eastern Europe and the Commonwealth of Independent States (CIS) region.

The two organisations believe that around 23 million hectares of arable land were withdrawn from production in recent years and that at least 13 million hectares could be returned to production with no major environmental cost, particularly in Russia, Ukraine and Kazakhstan.

In a speech delivered at the conference FAO Director-General Jacques Diouf called for courageous steps to be taken now to help unlock this untapped agricultural production potential, noting that current predictions for CIS grain production point to a rise of 7% to 159 million tonnes between 2007 and 2016.

EBRD President Jean Lemierre added: "There is now an urgent need for both the private and public sectors to work together to create the conditions for sustainable investment that will restore the primacy of this region as a crucial centre of agricultural production."

An EBRD paper submitted to the conference noted governments have responded to rising food prices by introducing a series of measures including price controls, increased subsidies, reduced import barriers and restrictions on exports designed to benefit consumers. The paper also noted that many of these measures, while well-intentioned, could prove to be counterproductive on a long-term basis.

Planting Financial Needs

Anton Usov, the EBRD's press officer in Ukraine, says that the new cooperation in the agricultural sector between EBRD and FAO is just getting under way and will probably be a major topic of discussion during EBRD's annual meeting, to be held in Kyiv in May this year.

Usov states that the EBRD has already made a considerable number of agribusiness loans in Ukraine and looks forward to expanding its interest in the field.

He pointed to a EUR [euro] 10 million loan that was closed in May 2007 to a primary agricultural producer, Agro-invest, part of MK Group—a leading producer and exporter of crop farming cultures in Serbia and one of the main agribusiness operators in Europe.

The funds are being used to develop a modern grain storage elevator in Ukraine with a capacity exceeding 100,000 tonnes, which will enable Agroinvest to store, dry and handle its own and third party grains in an efficient manner and provide the standardized quality of grain required by the market.

The EBRD paper encouraged governments to limit interventions that would distort domestic markets or disadvantage producers and traders, arguing that the most effective way to generate a supply response to the rise in global demand is to facilitate investment along the entire agricultural value chain.

Protection of the poorest consumers, it suggested, could be achieved through targeted income support to the most vulnerable segments of the population.

The Bank [EBRD] said it would target its own investments to the development of local supply chains to increase production and to the development of new rural financing instruments.

Yuriy Alatortsev, a Ukrainian agricultural analyst and writer, agreed. "We are stupid by paying farmers a fixed fee per hectare with prices skyrocketing. We should invest in technology and technical assistance instead."

Working to Improve Communication

In cooperation with the FAO, the EBRD will also pursue greater policy dialogue to help overcome the lack of communication and effective contact between private sector companies and related authorities in the agricultural sectors across the transition region. In the agribusiness sector alone, the EBRD has already committed EUR 4.9 billion in 357 projects across central and eastern Europe and the CIS.

In its submission to the conference, FAO spokesmen said ambitious government policies are vital, implying improved use of state budgets to deliver essential public goods and services to the agricultural sector.

"A supportive institutional and regulatory environment is mandatory to attract private investment at all levels of the food chain. To achieve that, improving policy dialogue between private stakeholders and policy makers will be instrumental."

No country in the world has a better opportunity to improve the food security of the world than Ukraine.

Alatortsev believes that the EBRD's commitment is commendable, but is far too small for the area that it proposes to serve. "More and more investment will be needed. Across all of the CIS, EUR 4.9 billion is nothing. Pretty soon private companies will invest billions of dollars into Ukrainian agriculture alone", Alatortsev said.

"No country in the world has a better opportunity to improve the food security of the world than Ukraine," Leonid Kozachenko said in a March 19 interview.

"Money is no longer the problem. Between commercially available sources and such entities as the EBRD and the IFC [International Finance Corporation], there are adequate supplies of funding.

"What we need to do is throw out old ideas, to understand that we can adequately supply domestic demand and the world market, and to sweep away the old thinking and the old laws and regulations that prevent Ukraine from regaining its place as one of the great breadbaskets of the world.

"I hope that we will have the courage and vision to grasp this immense opportunity that is clearly within our reach."

Periodical Bibliography

The following articles have been selected to supplement the diverse views presented in this chapter.

Richard Alleyne
"Food and Energy Shortages Will Create 'Perfect Storm', says Prof John Beddington," *Daily Telegraph* (UK), March 19, 2009.

Belfast Telegraph
"Grim Warning of Water and Food Shortages," March 20, 2009.

Jason Gerald
"PM: We Cannot Wait for Food Shortages to Occur," *New Straits Times* (Malaysia), April 21, 2008.

Louise Gray
"The Good Life Answer to a Food Shortage," *Daily Telegraph* (UK), September 29, 2008.

George Jacobs
"Meat the Culprit in Food Shortage," *Straits Times* (Singapore), April 8, 2008.

Jonathan Leake
"Food Shortages Loom as Wheat Crop Shrinks and Prices Rise," *Sunday Times* (UK), February 24, 2008.

Daniella Miletic
"Drought, Population and Biofuels Threaten Food Supplies," *The Age* (Melbourne, Australia), January 18, 2008.

Siti Nurbaiyah Nadznmi
"No Need to Panic over Rice Shortage," *New Straits Times* (Malaysia), April 13, 2008.

Chris Padley
"The Big Issue: Food Shortages, Population Control Must Not Be Ignored," *Observer* (UK), December 20, 2009.

Reuters Africa
"Eritrean President Says No Food Shortage in 2010," November 13, 2009. http://af.reuters.com.

CHAPTER 3

Human Health
and Food Safety

Nutritional Quality of Organic Foods: A Systematic Review[1-4]

Alan D. Dangour, Sakhi K. Dodhia, Arabella Hayter,
Elizabeth Allen, Karen Lock, and Ricardo Uauy

In the following viewpoint Alan D. Dangour and his colleagues at the London School of Hygiene & Tropical Medicine argue that there are no significant nutritional differences between organically grown and conventionally grown foods. Differences in organically grown foods that were detected are likely due to fertilizer use and conditions of the foods at harvest, but do not provide any further health benefits. The researchers make it clear that they did not study the impact of pesticides or other chemicals used in growing the foods under investigation.

As you read, consider the following questions:

1. About how much was the worldwide organic market worth in 2007?

2. Over what time frame did the authors collect the studies used in their viewpoint?

3. About how many nutrients or nutritionally relevant substances were identified by the authors' review?

Introduction

The demand for organically produced food is increasing. In 2007 the organic food market in the United Kingdom was es-

Alan D. Dangour, Sakhi K. Dodhia, Arabella Hayter, Elizabeth Allen, Karen Lock, and Ricardo Uauy, "Nutritional Quality of Organic Foods: A Systematic Review," *American Journal of Clinical Nutrition*, July 29, 2009. Copyright © 2009 by The American Society for Nutrition. Reproduced by permission.

timated to be worth >£2 billion, an increase of 22% since 2005 (1), and the global estimate was £29 billion (2). Organic foodstuffs are produced according to specified standards, which, among other factors, control the use of chemicals in crop production and medicines in animal production and emphasize a minimal environmental impact (3, 4). Previous nonsystematic reviews have concluded that organically produced foods have a nutrient composition superior to that of conventional foods (5–7), although this finding has not been consistent (8, 9). To date, there has been no systematic review of the available published literature on this topic.

All natural products vary in their composition of nutrients and other nutritionally relevant substances (10). Different cultivars of the same crop may differ in nutrient composition, which can also vary depending on fertilizer and pesticide regimen, growing conditions, season, and other factors. The nutrient composition of livestock products can similarly be affected by factors such as the age and breed of the animal, feeding regimen, and season. This inherent variability in nutrient content may be further affected during the storage, transportation, and preparation of the foodstuffs before they reach the plate of the consumer. (See Supplemental Figure 1 under "Supplemental data" in the online issue). An understanding of the factors that affect nutrient variability in crops and livestock products is important for the design and interpretation of research on differences in the nutrient content of organically produced and conventionally produced foodstuffs.

Notwithstanding the current uncertainty in the available evidence on the nutrient composition of foods produced under different agricultural regimens, consumers appear willing to pay a higher price for organic foods based on their perceived health and nutrition benefits (11, 12). Establishing the strength of existing evidence relating to the nutrient content of organic food will enable the development of evidence-based statements on content and potential nutrition-related public health gains or risks resulting from its consumption, which will allow consumers to make informed choices.

We present the results of a systematic review of studies that report the chemical analysis of foodstuffs produced under organic or conventional methods. The outcome was restricted to the nutrient and nutritionally relevant content of foodstuffs. We did not address differences in contaminant contents (e.g., herbicide, pesticide, or fungicide residues) or the possible environmental consequences of organic and conventional agricultural practices because this was beyond the scope of our review. . . .

Consumers appear willing to pay a higher price for organic foods based on their perceived health benefits.

Discussion

This report presents the results of the first published systematic review investigating differences in nutrient content of organically and conventionally produced foodstuffs. The review includes peer-reviewed publications published with an English abstract over the past 50 y[ears]. The organic movement has a long history (15), and the large proportion of articles identified in this review published after 2000 highlights the high level of current scientific interest.

The analysis presented suggests that organically and conventionally produced foods are comparable in their nutrient content. For 10 of 13 nutrient categories analyzed, there were no significant differences between production methods. Differences that were detected in crops were biologically plausible and were most likely due to differences in fertilizer use (nitrogen and phosphorus) (3) and ripeness at harvest (titratable acidity) (16). It is unlikely that consumption of these nutrients at the levels reported in organic foods in this study provide any health benefit. An important corollary is that organically produced foods are not inferior to conventionally produced foods with respect to their nutrient content.

Unlike all previous reviews that were nonsystematic, we conducted a rigorous literature search and identified a large number of studies conducted over the past 50 y[ears]. Our systematic approach, which focused on studies of satisfactory quality, agrees with some (higher contents of phosphorus in organic foods) but not all (higher contents of vitamin C and magnesium in organic foods) findings from previous reviews (5, 7, 9).

The analysis presented suggests that organically and conventionally produced foods are comparable in their nutrient content.

Results of analyses on >450 different nutrients or nutritionally relevant substances were identified in our review, and, whereas many articles appeared to have focused objectives guiding the analysis conducted and presented, others reported information on a considerable number of disparate substances. Given the large number of nutrients reported, we decided to group them into distinct nutrient categories for further analysis. We provided the totality of the data extracted from all satisfactory quality studies as a future resource for nutrition and agricultural researchers. (See Supplemental Tables 7 and 8 under "Supplemental data" in the online issue).

Our review again highlighted the heterogeneity and generally poor quality of research in this area (11). The criteria we used to assess publication quality were identified as key methodological components of study design, specifically relating to exposure (certification of organic production and definition of foodstuff) and outcome (statements on laboratory and statistical analysis methods). We attempted no further gradings within each quality criterion; e.g., organic certifying bodies have differing production regulations, and laboratory methods have different sensitivities (17). Despite the relatively low threshold used in this review to define satisfactory quality studies, a disappointingly low number of studies was graded as being of satisfactory quality. We urge researchers investigating nutritional characteristics of organic food to improve the scientific quality of their work and propose our five criteria as the bare minimum when reporting studies. To enable assessment of the nutritional quality of the foodstuffs in relation to their growing environment and mode of production, well-controlled long-term field trials, which provide explicit and detailed information on production methods, would be particularly valuable. An additional analysis including all 162 studies identified, irrespective of quality, similarly concluded that there was no evidence of important differences in nutrient content between organically and conventionally produced foodstuffs (data not shown).

This review had several strengths, such as its systematic and exhaustive nature, its broad inclusion criteria, and its methodological rigor. However, because of the limitations of the extracted data, no formal meta-analysis was possible. To make best use of the available data, we elected to combine results from different study designs and calculated standardized differences across foods by nutrient category. This will have resulted in the loss of the more nuanced findings from individual studies on specific foods but was chosen to be the most effective method for including and reporting all available data in a standardized form.

This review also had some limitations, which relate more specifically to the review process. We excluded gray literature and foreign language publications without English abstracts, and we were unable to locate a small number ($n = 11$) of potentially relevant publications, which may have resulted in us not including some relevant data in the review. Reporting bias, which occurs when authors do not report all analyses conducted in their research, and publication bias, which oc-

Comparison of Organic and Conventional Foods

Comparison of content of nutrients and other nutritionally relevant substances in organically and conventionally produced crops as reported in satisfactory quality studies

Nutrient category[1]	No. of studies	No. of comparisons	Results of Analysis		Higher levels in organic or conventional crops?
			Standardized difference[2] %	P	
Nitrogen	17	64	6.7 ± 1.9	0.003	Conventional
Vitamin C	14	65	2.7 ± 5.9	0.84	No difference
Phenolic compounds	13	80	3.4 ± 6.1	0.60	No difference
Magnesium	13	35	4.2 ± 2.3	0.10	No difference
Calcium	13	37	3.7 ± 4.8	0.45	No difference
Phosphorus	12	35	8.1 ± 2.6	0.009	Organic
Potassium	12	34	2.7 ± 2.4	0.28	No difference
Zinc	11	30	10.1 ± 5.6	0.11	No difference
Total soluble solids	11	29	0.4 ± 4.0	0.92	No difference
Copper	11	30	8.6 ± 11.5	0.47	No difference
Titratable acidity	10	29	6.8 ± 2.1	0.01	Organic

[1]Nutrient categories are listed by numeric order of the included studies. [2]All values are means ± SEs (robust).

TAKEN FROM: Alan D. Dangour, Sakhi K. Dodhia, Arabella Hayter, Elizabeth Allen, Karen Lock, and Ricardo Uauy, "Table 1: Comparison of content of nutrients and other nutritionally relevant substances in organically and conventionally produced crops as reported in satisfactory quality studies," *American Journal of Clinical Nutrition*, July 29, 2009. Copyright © 2009 by The American Society for Nutrition. Reproduced by permission.

curs when journal editors favor the publication of statistically significant findings are also potential limitations of systematic reviews (18). We are aware of 2 studies (19, 20) published after the review cutoff date.

There is no evidence to support the selection of organically produced foodstuffs over conventionally produced foodstuffs.

All natural products vary in their composition of nutrients and other nutritional relevant substances for a wide variety of reasons (10), including production method. Production methods, especially those that regulate the use of chemical fertilizer, herbicides, and pesticides may also affect the chemical content of foodstuffs. Certified organic regimens specify the production of foodstuffs with the strictly controlled use of chemicals and medicines. The potential for any benefits to public and environmental health of these actions would certainly warrant further systematic review, but was beyond the scope of the current report.

The current analysis suggests that a small number of differences in nutrient content exist between organically and conventionally produced foodstuffs and that, whereas these differences in content are biologically plausible, they are unlikely to be of public health relevance. One broad conclusion to draw from this review is that there is no evidence to support the selection of organically produced foodstuffs over conventionally produced foodstuffs to increase the intake of specific nutrients or nutritionally relevant substances. It is also clear that research in this area would benefit considerably from greater scientific rigor and a better understanding of the various factors (apart from production regimen) that determine the nutrient content of foodstuffs.

References

1. Soil Association. Soil Association organic market report 2007. Bristol, United Kingdom: Soil Association, 2007.

2. Datamonitor, Organic food: global industry guide. London, United Kingdom: Datarnonitor Ltd, 2008

3. European Community Council Regulation. Council Regulation (EC) no. 834/2007 of 28 June 2007 on organic production and labelling of organic products and repealing Regulation (EEC) no. 2092/91. In: EEC, ed. Official Journal of the European Union. Brussels, Belgium: European Community Council Regulation, 2007:1-23.

4. International Federation of Organic Agriculture Movements. The IFOAM norms for organic production and processing: version 2005. Bonn, Germany: International Federation of Organic Agriculture Movements, 2007.

5. Worthington V. Nutritional quality of organic versus conventional fruits, vegetables, and grains. J Altern Complement Med 2001;7:161-73.

6. Soil Association. Organic farming, food quality and human health: a review of the evidence. Bristol, United Kingdom: Soil Association, 2000.

7. Magkos F, Arvaniti F, Zampelas A. Organic food: nutritious food or food for thought? A review of the evidence. Int J Food Sci Nutr 2003;54:357-71.

8. Bourn D, Prescott J. A comparison of the nutritional value, sensory qualities, and food safety of organically and conventionally produced foods. Crit Rev Food Sci Nutr 2002;42:1-34.

9. Woese K, Lange D, Boess C, Bögl KW. A comparison of organically and conventionally grown foods—results of a review of the relevant literature. J Sci Food Agric 1999;74:281-93.

10. Food Standards Agency. McCance and Widdowson's the composition of foods. 6th summary edition. Cambridge, United Kingdom: Royal Society of Chemistry, 2002.

11. Williams CM. Nutritional quality of organic food: shades of grey or shades of green? Proc Nutr Soc 2002;61:19-24.

12. Winter CK, Davis SF. Organic foods. J Food Sci 2006;71:R117-24.

13. Stroup DF, Berlin JA, Morton SC, et al. Meta-analysis of observational studies in epidemiology: a proposal for reporting. Meta-analysis of Observational Studies in Epidemiology (MOOSE) group. JAMA 2000:283:2008-12.

14. World Cancer Research Fund, American Institute for Cancer Research. Food, nutrition, physical activity, and the prevention of cancer: a global perspective. Washington, DC: AICR. 2007.

15. Heckman J. A history of organic farming: transitions from Sir Albert Howard's War in the Soil to USDA National Organic Program. Renewable Agric Food Syst 2006;21:143-50.

16. Aherne SA, O'Brien NM. Dietary flavonols: chemistry, food content, and metabolism. Nutrition 2002;18:75-81.

17. Gibson RS. Principles of nutritional assessment. 2nd ed. Oxford, United Kingdom: Oxford University Press, 2005.

18. Higgins JPT, Green S, eds. Cochrane handbook for systematic review of interventions. Chichester, United Kingdom: John Wiley & Sons Ltd, 2008.

19. Butler G, Nielsen JH, Slots T. Fatty acid and fat-soluble antioxidant concentrations in milk from high- and

low-input conventional and organic systems: seasonal variation. J Sci Food Agric 2008;88:1431-41.

20. Roose M, Kahl J, Ploeger A. Influence of the farming system on the xanthophyll content of soft and hard wheat. J Agric Food Chern 2009;57:182-8.

Notes

1. From the Nutrition and Public Health Intervention Research Unit (ADD, SKD, AH, and RU) and the Medical Statistics Unit (EA), Department of Epidemiology and Population Health, London School of Hygiene & Tropical Medicine, London, United Kingdom, and the Health Services Research Unit, Department of Public Health and Policy, London School of Hygiene & Tropical Medicine, London, UK (KL).

2. The funding organization had no role in the study design, data collection, analysis, interpretation, or writing of the report. The review team held 6 progress meetings with the funding organization.

3. Supported by the UK Food Standards Agency (PAU221).

4. Address correspondence to AD Dangour, Nutrition and Public Health Intervention Research Unit, Department of Epidemiology and Population Health, London School of Hygiene & Tropical Medicine, Keppel Street, London WC1E 7HT, United Kingdom. E-mail: alan.dangour@lshtm.ac.uk.

Received May 7, 2009. Accepted for publication July 2, 2009.

doi: 10.3945/ajcn.2009.28041.

Organic Food Is Healthier for the World's Population

Charles Benbrook, Donald R. Davis, and Preston K. Andrews

Charles Benbrook, Donald R. Davis, and Preston K. Andrews are scientists who work for the Organic Consumers Association (OCA), an online, nonprofit organization campaigning for health, justice, and sustainability. In the following viewpoint, they argue that organic foods are healthier and more nutritious than conventionally grown foods. Benbrook and his colleagues dispute the findings of a recent study in the American Journal of Clinical Nutrition, *which shows that there is no difference between the two types of foods. They assert that the study ignores the actual nutritional values of some nutrients and includes data that has long been disproven.*

As you read, consider the following questions:

1. As explained in the viewpoint, why are elevated levels of nitrogen considered a health risk by most scientists?
2. How does the nutrient level in organic foods compare to the nutrient level in conventional foods, as asserted by the authors?
3. What five criteria does the Food Standards Agency (FSA) use to analyze its studies?

Charles Benbrook, Donald R. Davis, and Preston K. Andrews, "Organic Center Response to the FSA Study," Organic Consumers Association, July 2009. Reproduced by permission of The Organic Center.

An advance copy of a study appeared today [July 2009] that will be published in the September edition of the *American Journal of Clinical Nutrition*. The published paper, "Nutritional Quality of Organic Foods: A Systematic Review," was written by a team led by Alan [D.] Dangour, at the London School of Hygiene & Tropical Medicine and funded by the United Kingdom's Food Standards Agency (FSA).

In their written report, the London team downplayed positive findings in favor of organic food. In several instances, their analysis showed that organic foods tend to be more nutrient dense than conventional foods. Plus, their study omitted measures of some important nutrients, including total antioxidant capacity. It also lacked quality controls contained in a competing study released in 2008 by the Organic Center (TOC). Last, the FSA-funded team also used data from very old studies assessing nutrient levels in plant varieties that are no longer on the market.

Nutrient Levels

The London team reported finding statistically significant differences between organically and conventionally grown crops in three of 13 categories of nutrients. Significant differences cited by the team included nitrogen, which was higher in conventional crops, and phosphorus and tritratable acids, both of which were higher in the organic crops. Elevated levels of nitrogen in food are regarded by most scientists as a public health hazard because of the potential for cancer-causing nitrosamine compounds to form in the human GI tract. Hence, this finding of higher nitrogen in conventional food favors organic crops, as do the other two differences.

Despite the fact that these three categories of nutrients favored organic foods, and none favored conventionally grown foods, the London-based team concluded that there are no nutritional differences between organically and conventionally grown crops.

A team of scientists convened by the Organic Center (TOC) carried out a similar, but more rigorous, review of the same literature. The TOC team analyzed published research just on plant-based foods. Results differ significantly from the more narrow FSA review and are reported in the study "New Evidence Confirms the Nutritional Superiority of Plant-Based Organic Foods."

This finding of higher nitrogen in conventional foods favors organic crops.

The TOC findings are similar for some of the nutrients analyzed by the FSA team, but differ significantly for two critical classes of nutrients of great importance in promoting human health—total polyphenols and total antioxidant content. The FSA team did not include total antioxidant capacity among the nutrients studied, and it found no differences in the phenolic content in 80 comparisons across 13 studies.

Unlike the London study, the Organic Center review focused on nutrient differences in "matched pairs" of crops grown on nearby farms, on the same type of soil, with the same irrigation systems and harvest timing, and grown from the same plant variety. It also rigorously screened studies for the quality of the analytical methods used to measure nutrient levels, and eliminated from further consideration a much greater percentage of the published literature than the FSA team.

While the FSA team found 80 comparisons of phenolic compounds, the TOC team focused on the more precise measure of total phenolic acids, or total polyphenols, and found just 25 scientifically valid "matched pairs." By mixing together in their statistical analysis the results of several specific phenolic acids, the FSA team likely lost statistical precision.

Instead, the TOC team focused on studies reporting values for total phenolic acids, and also applied more rigorous selection criteria to exclude poorer quality studies.

The TOC team found—

Twenty-five matched pairs of organic and conventional crops for which total phenolic acid data was reported. The levels were higher in the organic crops in 18 of these 25 cases, conventional crops were higher in six. In five of the matched pairs, phenolic acid levels were higher in organic crops by 20% or more. On average across the 25 matched pairs, total phenolics were 10% higher in the organic samples, compared to conventional crops.

In seven of eight matched pairs reporting total antioxidant capacity data, the levels were higher in the organically grown crop. Of 15 matched pairs for the key antioxidant quercetin, 13 reported higher values in the organic food. In the case of kaempferol, another important antioxidant, the organic samples were higher in six cases, while five were higher in the conventional crops.

The consumption of organic fruits and vegetables, in particular, offered significant health benefits.

In the TOC study, there were an ample number of matched pairs to compare the levels of 11 nutrients, including five of the nutrients in the FSA review. For the five nutrients covered in each review, the TOC team was in general agreement with the FSA findings for two (nitrogen and phosphorus).

The London team did not assess differences in key individual antioxidants, nor in total antioxidant activity, important nutrients that have been measured in several more recent studies.

Across all the valid matched pairs and the 11 nutrients included in the TOC study, nutrient levels in organic food averaged 25% higher than in conventional food. Given that some

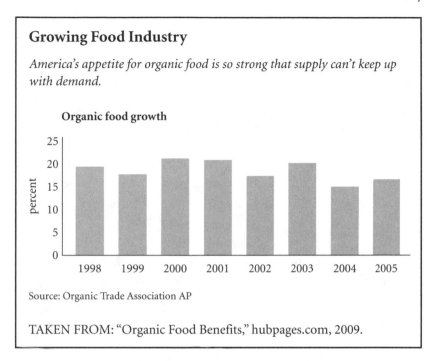

Growing Food Industry

America's appetite for organic food is so strong that supply can't keep up with demand.

Organic food growth

Source: Organic Trade Association AP

TAKEN FROM: "Organic Food Benefits," hubpages.com, 2009.

of the most significant differences favoring organic foods were for key antioxidant nutrients that most Americans do not get enough of on most days, the team concluded that the consumption of organic fruits and vegetables, in particular, offered significant health benefits, roughly equivalent to an additional serving of a moderately nutrient-dense fruit or vegetable on an average day.

Why the Different Results?

A review of the London-based team's methodology and study design points clearly to why the FSA and the Organic Center studies reached some different conclusions.

Inclusion of Older Studies. The FSA review included studies over a 50-year period: January 1958 through February 2008. The TOC team included studies published since 1980. Most studies published before 1980 were found flawed for purposes of comparing the nutrient content of today's conventional and organic crops.

Most of the older studies used plant varieties no longer in use, and did not measure or report total phenolics or antioxidant capacity (since these nutrients were just being discovered). The older studies used analytical methods that are now considered inferior, compared to modern methods.

Further, since the 1950s, plant breeders and growers have consistently increased the yields of food crops, leading, in some cases, to a dilution of nutrients. In 2004, one of us (Donald R. Davis) reported evidence for a general decline in some nutrient levels in 43 garden crops between 1950 and 1999.

Similarly, an Organic Center report by Brian Halweil describes in detail the evidence linking higher yields and nutrient decline. Thus, results in the FSA study are likely confounded by the team's decision to include data from over three decades ago.

Since the 1950s, plant breeders and growers have consistently increased the yields of food crops, leading, in some cases, to a dilution of nutrients.

New Studies Support Greater Nutrient Density in Organic Foods. Since February 2008, the cutoff date of the London study, some 15 new studies have been published, most of which use superior design and analytical methods based on criticisms of older studies. The Organic Center is updating its earlier analysis with these additional studies. These new studies generally reinforce the findings reported in the March 2008 TOC report, particularly in the case of nitrogen (higher in conventional crops, a disadvantage), and vitamin C, total phenolics, and total antioxidant capacity, which are typically higher in organically grown foods.

The center's study finds that protein content and beta-carotene, a precursor of vitamin A, are typically higher in conventionally grown foods, but since both are present at ample or excessive levels in the diets of most Americans, these differences do not confer a nutritional advantage nearly as important as heightened levels of phenolics and antioxidants in organic foods.

Exclusion of Studies Analyzing Results on "Integrated" Farms. The FSA team excluded studies comparing organic foods to "integrated" and biodynamic production systems, stating that "integrated" systems are not conventional. Most conventional U.S. fruit and vegetable producers are now using advanced levels of integrated pest management. Thus, "integrated" systems are now a more accurate description of "conventional" agriculture in the U.S., than a definition grounded in monoculture, the calendar spraying of pesticides, and excessive applications of chemical fertilizers. The London team did not report in the published paper which "integrated" studies were dropped, but we suspect some important U.S.-based studies may have been eliminated.

TOC Study Applied Much Stricter Screens for Scientific Validity. The two teams agree that many published studies are methodologically flawed, and hence should not be included in comparative studies. But the FSA and TOC teams used very different rules to screen studies for scientific quality and to select matched pairs for analyses.

The FSA team cites five criteria: definition of the organic system; specification of the plant variety (i.e., crop genetics); statement of nutrients analyzed; description of laboratory method used; and, a statement regarding statistical methods for assessing differences. The London team states that they simply required some discussion of these issues in published papers, but did not set or apply any qualitative thresholds in judging scientific validity.

The Organic Center team focused on the same factors (plus several others) and used stated, objective criteria for assessing them. The TOC team reviewed the statistical power and reliability of the analytical methods, a process that eliminated dozens of results. Finally, the TOC team insisted upon a close match of soils, plant genetics (variety), harvest method and timing, and irrigation systems, all factors that can bias the results of a comparison study.

Inclusion of Market Basket Studies. The FSA team included some market basket studies, for which there is no way to know the specific circumstances of the farm locations, the plant genetics, the soil type, or harvest method and timing. In the Organic Center study, market basket results were judged as "invalid" based on several quality-control screening criteria.

Preventing Illness from Listeria Infection in Canada Is Complicated

Michael Friscolanti

Michael Friscolanti is a senior writer at Maclean's *magazine, from which the following viewpoint is excerpted. He argues that determining how to prevent serious foodborne illnesses, like the Listeria outbreak that killed several people in Canada in 2008, is difficult. Listeria is a difficult bacterium to destroy, and it multiplies quickly, even under cold conditions. Ensuring high food processing standards is a way to reduce the amount and severity of future outbreaks, but most scientists agree that the potentially deadly contaminant will never be eradicated.*

As you read, consider the following questions:

1. How many people died from the Listeria outbreak in Canada in 2008?
2. How was the lethal strain of Listeria first discovered?
3. How often per year does the average person ingest L. mono, the deadly strain of Listeria?

The Clark family reunion was scheduled for the third weekend of July [2008]. Uncles and cousins and in-laws, from as far away as Utah and Florida, had marked the date on their

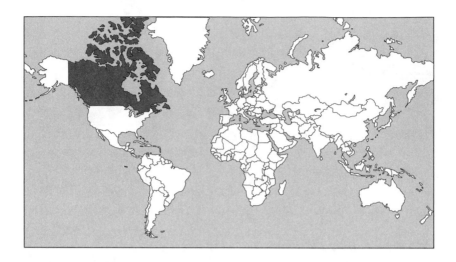

calendars months before. Plane tickets were booked, motel rooms were reserved, and the venue was set: Madoc, Ont. [Ontario, Canada], (population 2,044).

Frances Clark was at the centre of the plans. The matriarch of the clan baked some of her famous raspberry pies, froze a few pans of homemade lasagna, and spent weeks making sure the house—built by her late husband's grandfather in 1915—looked just right for the big party. "At breakfast one morning she said: 'You know, I'm going to go into the other room and work on that window,'" recalls her daughter Karen. "There was some caulking on the frame, and she wanted to dig it out so the window would go up and down for the reunion. You wouldn't believe that woman with a hammer. Mike Holmes had nothing on her." Frances Clark was 89 years old.

Later that morning, as she walked to her bedroom for a brief nap, Frances tripped and dislocated her left shoulder. When Karen came home from work, she found her mom lying on the floor, flat on her back. "I said: 'Mother, what are you doing down there?' She said: 'Well, I thought I'd lie here and count the ceiling tiles.' She was hilarious. Count the ceiling tiles? How many women, at 89, would say that?"

Frances spent the next four weeks at Belleville General Hospital. Although she missed the reunion, her out-of-town relatives made sure to stop by for a visit. After they left, Frances made a difficult decision: Maybe it's time I move into a nursing home. "She was transferred to Stirling Manor on Aug. 7," her daughter says. "She was making new friends, talking everyone's ear off. This was not some old lady who had lost her marbles and was tied up somewhere, drooling. Far from it."

An Unstoppable Bug

Two weeks later, Clark was back in a hospital bed, barely conscious and gasping for air. Her temperature skyrocketed, her eyes glazed over, and the antibiotics proved no match for the bacteria coursing through her body. "A couple of times she tried to say a word or two, but it was incomprehensible," says her son Tim. On Aug. 25, at 5:15 in the morning, Frances passed away. The official cause of death was listeriosis, a flu-like infection that attacks the central nervous system.

The experts have reached one uncomfortable conclusion: Listeria is unstoppable.

Today, Clark's family knows this much for sure: During her initial stay at the Belleville hospital, she was served Maple Leaf [Foods Inc.] "Sure Slice" ham (lot #21440) three separate times. After moving to the nursing home, she ate even more Maple Leaf lunch meat, including turkey and roast beef. "A double dose," Karen says. Those products, of course, were later recalled after lab tests revealed dangerously high levels of Listeria monocytogenes, the powerful pathogen that causes listeriosis. But for Clark—and 19 others killed by Maple Leaf meat—the recall came too late. She was in the last hours of her life, surrounded by children and grandchildren, when Michael McCain, the company president, went on television to apologize to the victims.

"To Canadians who are ill and to the families who have lost loved ones, I offer my deepest sympathies," said a sombre McCain. "Words cannot begin to express our sadness for your pain. Our best efforts failed, and we are deeply sorry."

Class action lawsuits have already been launched against Maple Leaf Foods Inc., demanding hundreds of millions of dollars for the company's alleged "negligence." Tim and Karen Clark are among the plaintiffs. "I'm sure Michael feels really bad about it, and I think his apology was very sincere," says Tim, who watched McCain's two paid commercials. "How this happened, who knows? But prevention is the key now. We want to make sure this doesn't happen again."

Keeping the food chain free of Listeria is a complicated, ever-evolving recipe of common sense, third-party oversight, targeted testing—and a dash of calculated risk.

So do the biologists, bureaucrats and every other food safety expert who has spent the past 30 years in a scientific wrestling match with this nasty little bug. But unfortunately, after countless case studies and many high-tech breakthroughs, the experts have reached one uncomfortable conclusion: Listeria is unstoppable. As much as the Clarks—and all Canadians—would like a foolproof fix, there isn't one. No matter what companies do, no matter how many safeguards they adopt, there will always be that chance, however slim, that your ham sandwich or your bagged lettuce or your brick of cheese contains a deadly helping of Listeria. "You're going to see another outbreak just like this one," says microbiologist F. Ann Draughon, co-director of the University of Tennessee's Food Safety Center of Excellence. "Listeriosis cases are decreasing, but there will be more outbreaks. It is inevitable."

That certainly doesn't exonerate Maple Leaf Foods. Their products killed 20 people (maybe more), sickened dozens of others, and made everyone else think twice about eating those cold cuts sitting in the fridge. But was the company negligent? That answer may be impossible to pin down. When it comes to Listeria control, the definition of "best efforts" is more a matter of scientific interpretation than undisputed fact.

Lowering the Odds of Infection

No one—not Maple Leaf, and not the federal government— can test every ounce of lunch meat before it leaves the plant. There would be nothing left to eat. The alternative, then, is an imperfect compromise that attempts to decrease the danger as much as possible while still ensuring that our supermarket shelves are sufficiently stocked. Keeping the food chain free of Listeria is a complicated, ever-evolving recipe of common sense, third-party oversight, targeted testing—and a dash of calculated risk. No two companies, or countries, follow the same playbook, and the debate over how best to battle this bacteria is still very much unsettled.

Can more be done to lower the odds of another Frances Clark dying? Absolutely. Are the experts unanimous on the best way to do that? Absolutely not.

Listeria is a microscopic, rod-shaped bacteria, and although it isn't visible to the naked eye, it is all around us. Soil, water, raw meat, your shoes. For the most part, the organism is harmless, except for that one particular species: Listeria mono-cytogenes [L. mono]. Ironically enough, L. mono was first identified as a foodborne pathogen in Canada, when a bad batch of coleslaw killed 17 people in 1981.

In the three decades since, much has been gleaned about the bug. It is strong, stubborn and sturdy enough to grow in cold temperatures. The bright side? Like salmonella or E. coli, it can be killed with heat. Cook your prime rib properly, and you'll be just fine.

However, ready-to-eat foods—the deli meats, fresh produce and boxed cereals that go straight from the grocery cart to your mouth—present a whole different challenge. They are designed to be eaten with no fuss and no preparation, so if they leave the factory laced with L. mono, those cells are going to end up in your stomach (unless you're among the small minority who fries his bologna).

Most of the time, though, a single serving won't require an ambulance. In fact, researchers believe the average person ingests L. mono every three or four days—that's 100 times a year—without ever realizing it. The reasons vary. For one, most people are naturally healthy enough to escape its wrath. L. mono also comes in dozens of different strains, and some are much more virulent than others. And sickness is a matter of dosage, not existence; most listeriosis victims ate foods that contain extremely high levels—well over 1,000 "colony forming units" (cfu) per gram.

Pregnant women are 20 times more likely to contract listeriosis, with side effect ranging from miscarriage to stillbirth.

"There is no such thing as a 100 per cent safe food product," says microbiologist Elliot T. Ryser, a foodborne diseases expert at Michigan State University. "But people are consuming Listeria on a regular basis, and we aren't dropping over like flies." Indeed. South of the border, the listeriosis rate is 2.7 cases per million people. In 2003 (the latest figures available) the number of confirmed cases in Canada was 59. Salmonella, on the other hand, infects up to 12,000 Canadians a year.

Still, those lopsided stats tell another, much more dire, story. Yes, listeriosis is responsible for only 0.02 per cent of all foodborne illnesses, but the fatality rate is extremely high, accounting for 28 per cent of all deaths from foodborne illness. This bitsy bacterium also attacks the most vulnerable: children, the elderly, and those with weak immune systems. Pregnant women are 20 times more likely to contract listeriosis, with side effects ranging from miscarriage to stillbirth. "My wife is seven months pregnant and she doesn't touch deli meats," says food scientist Doug Powell, director of the International Food Safety Network at Kansas State University. "But not everyone has a PhD in food science."

Adding to the complexity of Listeria control is the fact that most contaminated products don't start out that way. The cow or chicken that becomes your lunch meat, for example, is cleaned and cooked after slaughter, destroying most bacteria. Yet in the final stages of production, when the meat is sliced and packaged, it has the potential to become recontaminated by Listeria cells lurking in the factory. For ready-to-eat food companies, it is a never-ending game of seek and destroy. "This is an insidious organism that is very hardy and survives very nicely," says John Cerveny, now retired as manager of microbiology at Oscar Mayer, the U.S. firm famous for its hot dogs. "We're doing everything we can to minimize the problem, but we'll never eliminate it. Not in my lifetime."

The most frustrating fact about Listeria is that it multiples over time, even in a refrigerator.

Focusing on High-Risk Products

For Cerveny and his fellow scientists, the most frustrating fact about Listeria is that it multiplies over time, even in a refrigerator. If sliced turkey contains just a trace, that bacteria will inevitably reproduce, especially in an ideal breeding ground like moist, uncured cold cuts. Leave that same meat on a counter in room temperature, and the growth can be even more rapid—doubling in size every 15 minutes. Think about that. A one-gram piece that begins with 10 Listeria cells (an amount widely believed to be harmless) has the potential to reach 20 in just 15 minutes. In less than three hours, it can grow to 20,000—the same fatal dose discovered in some Maple Leaf products tested after the outbreak.

Who Is Responsible for Food Safety in Canada?

Achieving Food Safety

Industry
- Establishes and conducts food safety programs in accordance with regulatory requirements and industry practices
- Verifies effectiveness of food safety systems, and ensures safe production and distribution of food

Consumer
- Clean, washes hands with soap
- Handles, prepares and cooks food safely
- Consumes foods with caution

Local Public Health/ Regional Public Health Authorities
- Inspect food establishments
- Educate regarding food safety practices
- Report confirmed cases of foodborne illnesses to province/territory
- Investigate foodborne illness outbreaks; collect food samples; send samples to labs
- Conduct analyses of findings

Provincial/Territorial Governments
- Regulate food processing within their jurisdiction
- Implement food safety programs
- Lead outbreak investigations within their jurisdiction
- Communicate food safety messages to public

Federal Government

Canadian Food Inspection Agency (CFIA)
- Enforces all federal laws and regulations dealing with food
- Ensures industry compliance with food safety regulations through inspection/compliance verification of food producers
- Investigates food responsible for foodborne illness outbreaks with food safety partners
- Initiates food recalls (with industry)

Health Canada (HC)
- Sets food safety standards/policies
- Makes health risk assessment decisions re foods on market
- Communicates to public on food safety issues

Public Health Agency of Canada (PHAC)
- Acts as first point of contact for federal government for human health impact of foodborne outbreaks
- Conducts public health surveillance
- Leads epidemiological investigations when investigation is in more than one province

TAKEN FROM: "How Does Canada's Food Safety System Work?" www.canada.gc.ca, July 23, 2009.

It is no surprise, then, that Health Canada and the Canadian Food Inspection Agency (CFIA) focus their Listeria-fighting efforts on the highest-risk products. According to the current guidelines, foods that do not support the growth of Listeria and/or have a shelf life of less than 10 days (cereal, for example, or bagged salads) can contain up to 100 cfu per gram. However, those products that do support Listeria growth—lunch meat, hot dogs, soft cheeses and ready-made sandwiches—must be completely free of the pathogen. Even a smidgen will trigger a recall.

Those guidelines, however, are just that: guidelines. Despite its tough, zero-tolerance stance, even Health Canada concedes that up to 10 per cent of all ready-to-eat foods for sale right now contain some levels of L. mono. Reaching zero is simply not possible. It would be like trying to nab every last motorist who drives one kilometre over the speed limit.

An investigation ordered by Stephen Harper [prime minister of Canada] is in the works, but the prime suspect in the Maple Leaf outbreak has already been identified: two industrial-sized slicers at the company's Bartor Road factory in Toronto. Experts who inspected the plant after it shut down believe the bacteria was hiding "deep inside" the machines, thriving in hard-to-reach crevasses that weren't cleaned during routine sanitation. The company suspects the cells originated from one of four possible sources, including a drain or an elevator station, before slinking their way into the slicer.

The CFIA has since ordered every ready-to-eat meat company to conduct "a systematic and thorough cleaning" of all similar equipment. However, the much larger question still looms: How could so many cold cuts be so heavily contaminated and still get out the door without anybody noticing?

In the old days, inspectors focused on finding the bacteria where it mattered most: in the final product. Morsels from high-risk lots were tested for L. monocytogenes, and if found, the entire load was scrapped. But that method is far from perfect. Again, it isn't feasible to test every slice. The only alternative—random sampling—isn't fail-safe either, because Listeria lands sporadically, a few cells here, a few cells there. If you have a skid full of corned beef, for example, and only 1 per cent contains L. mono, you would need to test 299 samples to ensure a 95 per cent probability of discovering it—and even then, there is still that 5 per cent chance you won't find it.

Guided by those unsettling statistics, the modern-day protocol has evolved into an industry-wide system of good manufacturing practices (GMPs) verified by regular environmental sampling. Simply put, companies now swab their machines and their factories for signs of Listeria, with much less emphasis on the food itself. "The focus used to be: 'Let's test the dickens out of the finished product,'" says Jeffrey Kornacki, a Wisconsin microbiologist who has advised dozens of food companies. "But people have now realized that almost all the contamination of ready-to-eat foods is coming from the environment of the facility, so we have put an extreme emphasis on testing that." . . .

"I would not give [lunch meat] to a pregnant woman, I would not give it to small children, and I would not give it to the elderly."

Managing the Risk

As a society, we must also consider whose job it is to manage that risk. Is it Maple Leaf's responsibility to warn pregnant women to avoid lunch meat? Should cold cuts be banned from retirement home dining rooms? And what about butchers? Companies can do their darndest to keep Listeria out of their meat, but those slicers at the deli can easily recontaminate what was once a clean product. One recent study found that lunch meat purchased at your local deli counter is seven times more likely to contain Listeria than a sealed package straight from the factory.

And then there is this question, which most people rarely consider: If you leave your ham sandwich on the kitchen table all afternoon, and the Listeria cells double every 15 minutes, is that your fault or Michael McCain's?

"Educating consumers about these products is the most important thing," Draughon says. "As far as I'm concerned, these products should not be served in a nursing home, period. They are not appropriate for anybody who has impaired health, and I will argue with anyone all day long about that. I would not give it to a pregnant woman, I would not give it to small children, and I would not give it to the elderly. It's just too high risk a food—and I love my luncheon meats."

McCain says warning labels are "a debate worth having," but for now, his company plans to distribute information brochures to all nursing homes and hospitals that serve Maple Leaf goods. "The most important asset we have is the trust of our consumers, and they put their trust in us to perform," he says. "It's our obligation to respect that trust."

For Frances Clark's daughter, that trust has been forever shaken, regardless of how many brochures the company prints. Karen Clark says she will never again buy Maple Leaf products. In fact, since the day her mom died, she can't look at a grocery store shelf without wondering the worst. "You never questioned the safety of your food," she says. "You just assumed it was good."

Eating Meat Is Unhealthy and Contributes to the World Food Crisis

Chris Brazier

In the following viewpoint Chris Brazier, a co-editor at the New Internationalist, *argues the eating meat is not only unhealthy for human beings, but it also has negative consequences for the environment and contributes to the world food shortage. Brazier contends that Westerners have increased their consumption of meat over the past half a century, which has lead to an increase in greenhouse gases and other environmental hazards due to the livestock industry. In addition, Brazier argues that eating meat places a burden on world food offerings by limiting the amount of land on which fruits, vegetables, and grains can be grown.*

As you read, consider the following questions:

1. According to a 2007 survey, what percentage of Britons are vegan?
2. According to the author, what percentage of greenhouse gas emissions can be attributed to livestock production?
3. How many tons of meat did farmers produce in 2006?

When I first became a vegetarian 30 years ago, I used to find myself in passionate discussions about food issues all the time. The situation seemed so urgent. There were so many reasons to be vegetarian that I felt (and still feel) that the burden of justification should be turned around—not 'why are you vegetarian?' but rather 'why on earth do you eat meat?' There were reasons of dietary health—avoiding fat and cholesterol—and distaste for the idea of feeding on the flesh of another sentient being. But those rarely cut any ice with committed meat-eaters. There was also my abhorrence of the treatment of animals in factory farming. However, if I chose the ground on which to do battle, I tended to talk about the misuse of food resources in a world where people still went hungry—the enormous amounts of grain and pulses fed to cattle to produce a much smaller amount of beef. I saw eschewing meat as 'a conscientious objection to a system with waste at one end and starvation at the other'.

Distasteful and Unnatural

In more recent years, whether because I have become more mellow (or more cowardly) with age, I have rarely ended up in such arguments. I have retained my convictions and my diet and have raised children for whom vegetarianism seems to be a fundamental part of their identity. I had expected at least one of them to experiment during adolescence, but instead they still perceive eating meat as both distasteful and unnatural.

Parenthood tends to focus you inward more, and to put you less in the paths of strangers to whom an 'abnormal' diet would need explaining. Friends and family already know where I am coming from. Extraordinarily, given the shocked disbelief when I first made my stand all those years ago, my extended family now splits pretty much down the middle (turkey-eaters were actually a minority last Christmas). Less surprisingly, the New Internationalist co-operative also now splits down the middle. When I first joined in 1984, I was profoundly shocked to find I was the lone vegetarian.

On the other hand, many friends who once seemed just as committed have reverted to eating meat, while in society as a whole vegetarians and vegans remain a small minority. In Britain a November 2007 survey by the Department for Environment, Food and Rural Affairs showed two per cent to be vegan, three per cent vegetarian and a further five per cent restricting themselves to fish or chicken. In other Western countries vegetarians and vegans are an even smaller minority.

Turning Point

But a sea change is now taking place. A turning point came when it became evident that the livestock industry, in addition to all its other failings, was a major contributor to climate change. Over the last year [2008], a crisis in the existing world food and farming model has erupted—refocusing attention on precisely those arguments about misuse of resources that fuelled my original concern.

The burden of justification should be turned around—not 'why are you vegetarian?' but rather 'why on earth do you eat meat?'

A turning point came when it became evident that the livestock industry . . . was a major contributor to climate change.

The 2006 report of the UN [United Nations] Food and Agriculture Organization (FAO), *Livestock's Long Shadow*, helped bring the global warming effect of the meat and dairy industries to public notice. Written by agricultural economist Dr. Henning Steinfeld, the report caused consternation in the livestock industry and cost the FAO some of its funding. More recently, in September 2008, Dr. Rajendra Pachauri, the chair of the Intergovernmental Panel on Climate Change, added his own fuel to this particular fire with a presentation in London. Though he was making a personal case rather than represent-

Global Meat Consumption per Head (kg per annum)		
	40 years ago	Now
US	89	124
Spain	22	119
Europe	56	89
Brazil	39	68
China	4	54
Japan	8	42

TAKEN FROM: Chris Brazier, "Meat's Too Expensive," *New Internationalist*, no. 418, December 2008.

ing his organization, there were inevitably newspaper headlines along the lines of 'UN chief says eat less meat to stop global warming'.

His presentation encompassed the latest statistics, gathered from a range of different sources, not only on greenhouse gas emissions from the livestock industry, but on the wasteful inefficiency of a food and farming model based on meat and dairy produce. Among the key facts he included were:

- Livestock production accounts for 80 per cent of greenhouse gas emissions from agriculture and for 18 per cent of all greenhouse gas emissions from human activities—including 37 per cent of the methane (23 times the global warming potential of CO_2 [carbon dioxide] over 100 years), and 65 per cent of the nitrous oxide (265 times the global warming potential of CO_2 over 100 years).

- Producing one kilogram of beef leads to the emission of greenhouse gases with a warming potential equivalent to 36.4 kilograms of CO_2—equivalent to the amount emitted by the average European car every 250 kilometres. The production of that one kilo of beef consumes 169 megajoules of energy—enough to light a 100-watt bulb for 20 days.

- On top of this, meat requires refrigerated transportation and storage, extensive packaging and cooking at high temperatures for long periods. A high proportion of meat (bones and fat, as well as past-sell-by-date products) is wasted and finds its way into landfills or incinerators.

- A farmer can feed up to 30 people throughout the year on one hectare with vegetables, fruits, cereals and vegetable fats. If the same area is used for the production of meat, milk or eggs, the number of persons fed varies from five to 10.

- A third of the world's cereal harvest and over 90 per cent of soya is used for animal feed, despite inherent inefficiencies. Yet it takes more than 10 kilograms of grain to produce one kilo of beef, 4–5.5 kilos to produce one kilo of pork and 2.1–3.3 kilos of grain to produce one kilo of poultry meat.

- A vegan living for 70 years will pump an average of 100 tons less CO_2-equivalent into the atmosphere than someone eating meat and dairy products. . . .

The era of cheap, mass-produced food—dependent on the consumption of enormous amounts of energy and responsible for huge greenhouse gas emissions—is surely coming to an end. Yet meat eating worldwide continues to rise.

A vegan living for 70 years will pump an average of 100 tons less CO_2-equivalent into the atmosphere than someone eating meat and dairy products.

In 2006, farmers produced 276 million tons of meat, five times as much as in the 1950s. In the West, meat consumption has continued to increase, while those developing countries that have prospered over the period have immediately tended to mark their new prosperity by eating more meat—a trend that is obviously likely to continue.

To feed the projected extra demand, there would need to be a further doubling of meat and dairy production by 2050, involving a doubling in the number of farm animals from the current 60 billion to 120 billion. Yet 70 per cent of all agricultural land and 30 per cent of the world's surface land area is already given over to livestock.

These global eating trends are clearly unsustainable, whether in terms of producing (and sharing) enough food to feed a still-growing world population or of reducing greenhouse gas emissions. People who have up to now dismissed vegetarianism and veganism as mere 'lifestyle choices' may over the next few years be forced to think again. Governments will surely be required to intervene to reduce (or at least limit the growth in) the consumption of meat and dairy products. A good start would be eliminating the vast government subsidies from which the meat and dairy industries currently benefit.

At an individual level, altering our diet may be as much of a necessity in the years to come as insulating our homes or reducing our air travel. For those not prepared to give it up altogether, perhaps more attention could be paid to meat's origin—to eating only animals that have grazed areas unsuitable for arable farming. Or perhaps meat might return to being something saved for special occasions, for high days and holidays—as it was for earlier generations, and still is in most parts of the majority world. I felt the situation was urgent 30 years ago, but it is much more so now. The politics of food have always been emotive, but the stakes just got much, much higher.

Periodical Bibliography

The following articles have been selected to supplement the diverse views presented in this chapter.

Neels Blom	"South Africa: Technology Sows Seeds of Public Mistrust," *Business Day*, March 4, 2008.
Sylvain Charlebois	"Listeria Hysteria Can't Hurt," *Globe and Mail* (Canada), August 27, 2008.
Consumer Reports	"Lax Rules, Risky Food," January 2010.
Bryan Delaney	"Strategies to Evaluate the Safety of Bioengineered Foods," *International Journal of Toxicology*, vol. 26, no. 5, September 2007.
Farmers Guardian	"Consumers Less Concerned About Country of Origin," February 29, 2008.
Bae Ji-sook	"Civic Group Calls for Stronger GMO Rules," *Korea Times*, February 2, 2009.
Mustapha Kamil	"No Country Can Escape Price Rise," *New Straits Times* (Malaysia), April 21, 2008.
Lee Min-jai	"Beware GMO Produce," *Korea Times*, February 25, 2009.
Kate Phillips	"European Food Safety Group Calls for More Data on Additives," *Chemical Week*, August 25, 2008.
Karen Richardson	"Food Shortage Recasts Image of 'Organic,'" *Wall Street Journal*, June 25, 2008.
Alex Scott and Kate Phillips	"EU Consumer Group Aims to Ban Certain Colorants," *Chemical Week*, April 28, 2008.
Jeff Wells	"GMOS Revisited: Dissent Is Increasing," *Supermarket News*, April 28, 2008.

CHAPTER 4

Food and the World Economy

Removing U.S. Trade Barriers on Agricultural Exports from Developing Countries Benefits Domestic and Foreign Economies

David Beckmann

In the following viewpoint, David Beckmann argues that the world food crisis can be eliminated if countries providing aid to developing countries invest in agricultural development more than in food aid. In addition, this investment should be coupled with trade policies that support it, rather than hinder it. Current trade barriers exact much more in tariffs from developing countries than is given to them in aid. Removing the trade barriers would allow aid funds to work more effectively as well as enable farmers in developing countries to compete more effectively and to work their way out of poverty and alleviate the current food crisis. David Beckmann is a Lutheran pastor, an economist, and president of Bread for the World.

As you read, consider the following questions:

1. Beckmann says what percentage fewer calories does the average 2009 El Salvador meal have than the 2006 meal?

David Beckmann, "Meal Plan: How to Address the World Food Crisis," *Commonweal*, vol. 136, no. 11, 2009, pp. 7ff. Copyright © 2009 Commonweal Publishing Co., Inc. Reproduced by permission of Commonweal Foundation.

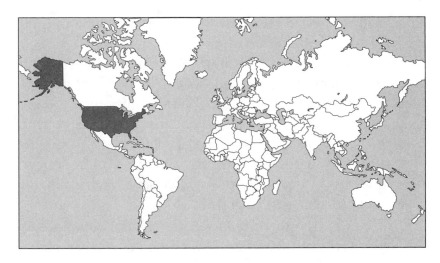

2. According to the author, why can't farmers in developing countries increase production to meet the present food crisis?

3. How do trade barriers contribute to the food crisis, according to Beckmann?

In the morning, eight-year-old Jorge Luis Hernandez has a small bowl of rice before going to work picking coffee beans near his home in the mountains of El Salvador. While attending school in the afternoon, he eats a meal of rice, beans, and tortillas, provided by the World Food Programme (WFP). It's his only full meal of the day. "Of course I am happy when I eat," he says. "When I'm hungry, my stomach hurts, I don't feel like playing, I don't feel like doing anything."

Jorge Luis Hernandez is not alone. Rising food prices in the United States have strained the budgets of many families. For poor people in developing countries, such increases have been devastating. WFP estimates that, as a result of skyrocketing prices, an average family meal in rural El Salvador today [2009] has 40 percent fewer calories than it did in May 2006. Worldwide, it is estimated the food crisis has pushed an additional 130 million people into poverty. Nearly 1 billion people do not know where their next meal will come from.

The food emergency of the past two years imperils decades of dramatic progress made against hunger and poverty. Since 1980, the percentage of people in the developing world living in extreme poverty has fallen from 50 to 25 percent. The percentage of undernourished people in the world declined from 28 to about 18 percent. But the worldwide food crisis threatens to undo that progress. More alarming still, the crisis could become permanent.

While it is true that prices for agricultural commodities are lower now than they were a year ago, they remain higher than they have been in decades, squeezing millions of people who already spend up to 80 percent of their income on food. Faced with the higher prices, poor people have to make difficult decisions. They limit the amount of food they consume, forgo meals, and reduce other expenditures such as health care or sending their children to school. The poorest people are coping by shifting to one meal a day and by eating famine foods: roots, grass, mud cakes.

So far, the world has dealt with this crisis primarily by increasing food aid. But while direct food aid saves lives in the short term, it can also feed a cycle of aid dependency and dampen prospects for long-term self-sufficiency.

The poorest people are coping by shifting to one meal a day and by eating famine foods: roots, grass, mud cakes.

To address the underlying conditions that drove prices up so dramatically, agriculture ministers from the Group of Eight (G8) countries, joined by their counterparts in China, India, Mexico, and Brazil, gathered in April. Their conclusion: Without immediate interventions in agriculture, the present food crisis could become structural in only a few decades. This would have serious consequences for the security and stability of world politics. The ministers issued a call to world leaders to put agriculture and food security at the center of the international agenda. To avert a permanent food shortage, they warned, global agricultural production must double by 2050. If new investments are made in global agriculture, the current crisis could be transformed into an opportunity for the world's poorest people.

Three-quarters of the world's hungry people live in rural areas in developing countries. They rely on agriculture for their livelihood. Greater agricultural production in these regions, particularly in Africa and Asia, could lead many families toward self-sufficiency and these poorer countries toward greater abundance. But most farmers there do not have the capacity to respond to the present crisis by simply planting more. For decades, bilateral and multilateral donors did not invest enough of their aid in agriculture. Too little was done to improve the necessary physical and technical infrastructure—rural transportation networks, storage facilities, irrigation systems, appropriate farming tools, agriculture extension services, and improved seed varieties. Support for agriculture as part of U.S. official development assistance has also declined. It was $8 billion in 1984; now it is less than half that amount. But even in 1984, foreign assistance neglected investments in agriculture development, instead favoring rapid, short-term responses to humanitarian crises and perceived national security threats.

Still, there is ample proof that large gains can be made in the fight against hunger and poverty through agricultural development. Vietnam, for instance, has had a tremendous growth spurt since the early 1990s. Extreme poverty declined from 58 percent of the population in 1993 to 16 percent in 2006. Vietnam's progress is due to a combination of economic reforms and technological innovations in its agricultural sector. Farmers responded, and from 1993 to 2006, per capita food production grew at 3.8 percent per year, a growth rate equaled or surpassed by only five countries in the world.

The [Barack] Obama administration has signaled a commitment to long-term investments in international agricultural development. Shortly before the G8 agriculture ministers' meeting in April, President Barack Obama asked Congress to double assistance for agriculture in developing countries to $1 billion, in addition to nearly $448 million for countries affected by the food and financial crisis. In Congress, attention to global agriculture development has been growing as well. The bipartisan Global Food Security Act, which authorizes additional resources for agriculture and rural development, unanimously passed the Senate Foreign Relations Committee in April.

In a time of economic hardship here and abroad, it is even more urgent that we use aid dollars well and direct more of our foreign assistance to programs that will help hungry people climb out of poverty.

Increasing food production alone, however, will not provide global food security. It must be coupled with trade policies that reinforce, rather than undercut, financial commitments to agriculture in places threatened by food insecurity. Farmers in developing countries could increase their earnings if they did not have to compete with subsidized crops from the United States and other industrialized countries. More could work their way out of poverty if rich countries fully opened their markets to agricultural exports from developing countries. The U.S. government applies the highest trade barriers to imports from the poorest countries—often the very same countries that receive U.S. development assistance. For example, in 2006, Bangladesh received $80 million in U.S. assistance, while the United States collected $487 million in tariffs on imports from Bangladesh.

Years of dwindling investments for agriculture and inconsistent trade policies reflect flaws in the overall system of U.S. development assistance. Our nation's global development policies are still driven by the 1961 Foreign Assistance Act. Programs are scattered across twelve departments, twenty-five different agencies, and nearly sixty government offices. A more efficient foreign-assistance system—with better coordination, accountability, and clarity—would allow people to get help faster and more effectively.

This year Congress and the administration should reframe foreign assistance to make it more effective in reducing poverty. Bipartisan legislation has been introduced in the House of Representatives as a first step toward a new Foreign Assistance Act—one that would help confront today's world food emergency with twenty-first-century solutions. In a time of economic hardship here and abroad, it is even more urgent that we use aid dollars well and direct more of our foreign assistance to programs that will help hungry people climb out of poverty.

Global Food Prices Rise with the Cost of Energy

Joachim von Braun

Joachim von Braun, is the director general of the International Food Policy Research Institute (IFPRI), a nonprofit organization that conducts research on agriculture policy issues. In the following viewpoint, von Braun argues that as the cost of energy rises, so does the cost of food. Biofuels, in particular, place a special burden on the world's food supply and limit the supply of food available, which raises the cost. The poorest countries are hurt most by these higher food prices, von Braun contends, forcing many people to live on foods of lesser nutritional quality.

As you read, consider the following questions:

1. How have the prices of milk and butter changed since the beginning of 2000?

2. According to the viewpoint, by what percentage are grain prices expected to increase over the next few years?

3. How low is global food aid support, as stated in the viewpoint?

World cereal and energy prices are becoming increasingly linked. Since 2000, the prices of wheat and petroleum have tripled, while the prices of corn and rice have almost doubled. The impact of cereal price increases on food-insecure and poor households is already quite dramatic. For every 1-percent increase in the price of food, food consumption expenditure in developing countries decreases by 0.75 percent. Faced with higher prices, the poor switch to foods that have lower nutritional value and lack important micronutrients.

Due to government price policies, trade restrictions, and transportation costs, changes in world commodity prices do not automatically translate into changes in domestic prices. In the case of Mexico, the margin between domestic and world prices for maize has ranged between 0 and 35 percent since the beginning of 2004, and a strong relationship between domestic and world prices is evident. In India, the differences between domestic and international rice prices were greater, averaging more than 100 percent between 2000 and 2006. While domestic price-stabilization policies diminish price volatility, they require fiscal resources and cause additional market imperfections. Government policies also change the relationship between consumer and producer prices. For instance, producer prices of wheat in Ethiopia increased more than consumer prices from 2000 to 2006.

Consumers in low-income countries are much more responsive to price changes than consumers in high-income countries.

Though international price changes do not fully translate into equivalent domestic farm and consumer price changes because of the different policies and trade positions adopted by each country, they are in fact transmitted to consumers and producers to a considerable extent.

The prices of commodities used in biofuel production are becoming increasingly linked with energy prices. In Brazil, which has been a pioneer in ethanol production since the 1970s, the price of sugar is very closely connected to the price of ethanol. A worrisome implication of the increasing link between energy and food prices is that high energy-price fluctuations are increasingly translated into high food-price fluctuations. In the past five years, price variations in oilseeds and in wheat and corn have increased to about twice the levels of previous decades.

The increasing demand for high-value commodities has resulted in surging prices for meat and dairy products, and this is driving feed prices upward, too. Since the beginning of 2000, butter and milk prices have tripled and poultry prices have almost doubled.

The effects of price increase on consumption are different across different countries and consumer groups. Consumers in low-income countries are much more responsive to price changes than consumers in high-income countries. Also, the demand for meat, dairy, fruits, and vegetables is much more sensitive to price, especially among the poor, than is the demand for bread and cereals.

The Effect of Biofuels

When oil prices range between US$60 and $70 a barrel, biofuels are competitive with petroleum in many countries, even with existing technologies. Efficiency benchmarks vary for different biofuels, however, and ultimately, production should be established and expanded where comparative advantages exist. With oil prices above US$90, the competitiveness is of course even stronger.

Feedstock represents the principal share of total biofuel production costs. For ethanol and biodiesel, feedstock accounts for 50–70 percent and 70–80 percent of overall costs, respectively. Net production costs—which are all costs related to production, including investments—differ widely across countries. For instance, Brazil produces ethanol at about half the cost of Australia and one-third the cost of Germany. Significant increases in feedstock costs (by at least 50 percent) in the past few years impinge on comparative advantage and competitiveness. The implication is that while the biofuel sector will contribute to feedstock price changes, it will also be a victim of these price changes.

Food-price projections have not yet been able to fully take into account the impact of biofuels expansion. When assessing potential developments in the biofuels sector and their consequences, the OECD-FAO [Organisation for Economic Cooperation and Development-Food and Agriculture Organization of the United Nations] outlook makes assumptions for a number of countries, including the United States, the European Union, Canada, and China. New biofuel technologies and policies are viewed as uncertainties that could dramatically impact future food prices. The Food and Agricultural Policy Research Institute (FAPRI) conducts a detailed analysis of the potential impact of policy on biofuels and links between the ethanol and gasoline markets, but its extensive modeling is limited to the United States.

A new, more comprehensive global scenario analysis using IFPRI's [International Food Policy Research Institute's] International Model for Policy Analysis of Agricultural Commodities and Trade (IMPACT) examines current price effects and estimates future ones. In view of the dynamic world food situation and the rapidly changing biofuels sector, IFPRI continuously updates and refines its related models, so the results presented here should be viewed as work in progress. Recently, the IMPACT model has incorporated 2005/06 developments in supply and demand, and has generated two future scenarios based on these developments:

- *Scenario 1* is based on the actual biofuel investment plans of many countries that have such plans and assumes biofuel expansions for identified high-potential countries that have not specified their plans.

- *Scenario 2* assumes a more drastic expansion of biofuels to double the levels used in Scenario 1.

The increase in crop prices resulting from expanded biofuel production is also accompanied by a net decrease in the availability of and access to food.

Under the planned biofuel expansion scenario (Scenario 1), international prices increase by 26 percent for maize and by 18 percent for oilseeds. Under the more drastic biofuel expansion scenario (Scenario 2), maize prices rise by 72 percent and oilseeds by 44 percent.

Under both scenarios, the increase in crop prices resulting from expanded biofuel production is also accompanied by a net decrease in the availability of and access to food, with calorie consumption estimated to decrease across all regions compared to baseline levels. Food-calorie consumption decreases the most in sub-Saharan Africa, where calorie availability is projected to fall by more than 8 percent if biofuels expand drastically.

One of the arguments in favor of biofuels is that they could positively affect net carbon emissions as an alterative to fossil fuels. That added social benefit might justify some level of subsidy and regulation, since these external benefits would not be internalized by markets. However, potential forest conversion for biofuel production and the impact of biofuel production on soil fertility are environmental concerns that require attention. As is the case with any form of agricultural production, biofuel feedstock production can be managed in sustainable or in damaging ways. Clear environment-related efficiency criteria and sound process standards need to be established that internalize the positive and negative externalities of biofuels and ensure that the energy output from biofuel production is greater than the amount of energy used in the process. In general, subsidies for biofuels that use agricultural production resources are extremely anti-poor because they implicitly act as a tax on basic food, which represents a large share of poor people's consumption expenditures and becomes even more costly as prices increase. . . .

Great technological strides are expected in biofuel production in the coming decades. New technologies converting cellulosic biomass to liquid fuels would create added value by both utilizing waste biomass and by using less land resources. These second-generation technologies, however, are still being developed and third-generation technologies (such as hydrogene) are at an even earlier phase. Even though future technology development will very much determine the competitiveness of the sector, it will not solve the food-fuel competition problem. The trade-offs between food and fuel will actually be accelerated when biofuels become more competitive relative to food and when, consequently, more land, water, and capital are diverted to biofuel production. To soften the trade-offs and mitigate the growing price burden for the poor, it is necessary to accelerate investment in food and agricultural science and technologies, and the CGIAR [Consultative Group on International Agricultural Research] has a vital role to play in this. For many developing countries, it would be appropriate to wait for the emergence of second-generation technologies, and "leapfrog" onto them later.

Predicting Food Price Changes

How will food prices change in coming years? This is one of the central questions that policy makers, investors, speculators, farmers, and millions of poor people ask. Though the research community does its best to answer this question, the many uncertainties created by supply, demand, market functioning, and policies mean that no straightforward answer can be given. However, a number of studies have analyzed the forces

Net Cereal Exports and Imports for Selected Countries (three-year averages 2003–2005)

Country	1000 tons
Japan	−24,986
Mexico	−12,576
Egypt	−10,767
Nigeria	−2,927
Brazil	−2,670
China	−1,331
Ethiopia	−789
Burkina Faso	29
India	3,637
Argentina	20,431
United States	76,653

Source: Data from FAO 2007a.

TAKEN FROM: International Food Policy Research Institute, "The World Food Situation: New Driving Forces and Required Actions," December 2007.

driving the current increases in world food prices and have predicted future price developments.

The Economist Intelligence Unit predicts an 11-percent increase in the price of grains in the next two years and only a 5-percent rise in the price of oilseeds. The OECD-FAO outlook has higher price projections (it expects the prices of coarse grains, wheat, and oilseeds to increase by 34, 20, and 13 percent, respectively, by 2016–17). The Food and Agricultural Policy Research Institute (FAPRI) expects increases in corn demand and prices to last until 2009–10, and thereafter expects corn production growth to be on par with consumption growth. FAPRI does not expect biofuels to have a large impact on wheat markets and predicts that wheat prices will stay constant due to stable demand as population growth offsets declining per capita consumption. Only the price of palm oil—

another biofuel feedstock—is projected to dramatically increase by 29 percent. In cases where demand for agricultural feedstock is large and elastic, some experts expect petroleum prices to act as a price floor for agricultural commodity prices. In the resulting price corridor, agricultural commodity prices are determined by the product's energy equivalency and the energy price.

The preliminary model results indicate that food prices would remain at high levels for quite some time.

In order to model recent price developments, changes in supply and demand from 2000 to 2005 as well as biofuel developments were introduced into the IFPRI IMPACT model (see Scenario 1). The results indicate that biofuel production is responsible for only part of the imbalances in the world food equation. Other supply and demand shocks also play important roles. The price changes that resulted from actual supply and demand changes during 2000–2005 capture a fair amount of the noted increase in real prices for grains in those years. For the period from 2006 to 2015, the scenario suggests further increases in cereal prices of about 10 to 20 percent in current U.S. dollars. Continued depreciation of the U.S. dollar—which many expect—may further increase prices in U.S.-dollar terms.

The results suggest that changes on the supply side (including droughts and other shortfalls and the diversion of food for fuel) are powerful forces affecting the price surge at a time when demand is strong due to high income growth in developing countries. Under a scenario of continued high income growth (but no further supply shocks), the preliminary model results indicate that food prices would remain at high levels for quite some time. The usual supply response embedded in the model would not be strong enough to turn matters around in the near future.

Who Benefits and Who Loses from High Prices?

An increase in cereal prices will have uneven impacts across countries and population groups. Net cereal exporters will experience improved terms of trade, while net cereal importers will face increased costs in meeting domestic cereal demand. There are about four times more net cereal-importing countries in the world than net exporters. Even though China is the largest producer of cereals, it is a net importer of cereals due to strong domestic consumption. In contrast, India—also a major cereal producer—is a net exporter. Almost all countries in Africa are net importers of cereals.

Price increases also affect the availability of food aid. Global food aid represents less than 7 percent of global official development assistance and less than 0.4 percent of total world food production. Food aid flows, however, have been declining and have reached their lowest level since 1973. In 2006, food aid was 40 percent lower than in 2000. Emergency aid continues to constitute the largest portion of food aid. Faced with shrinking resources, food aid is increasingly targeted to fewer countries—mainly in sub-Saharan Africa—and to specific beneficiary groups.

Price increases also affect the availability of food aid.

At the microeconomic level, whether a household will benefit or lose from high food prices depends on whether the household is a net seller or buyer of food. Since food accounts for a large share of the poor's total expenditures, a staple-crop price increase would translate into lower quantity and quality of food consumption. Household surveys provide insights into the potential impact of higher food prices on the poor. Surveys show that poor net buyers in Bolivia, Ethiopia, Bangladesh, and Zambia purchase more staple foods than net sellers sell. The impact of a price increase is country and crop specific. For instance, two-thirds of rural households in Java own between 0 and 0.25 hectares of land, and only 10 percent of households would benefit from an increase in rice prices.

In sum, in view of the changed farm-production and market situation that the poor face today, there is not much supporting evidence for the idea that higher farm prices would generally cause poor households to gain more on the income side than they would lose on the consumption-expenditure side. Adjustments in the farm and rural economy that might indirectly create new income opportunities due to the changed incentives will take time to reach the poor.

Choosing Locally Grown Foods Can Help Boost the Global Economy

Helena Norberg-Hodge and Steven Gorelick

Helena Norberg-Hodge and Steven Gorelick are the authors of Bringing the Food Economy Home: Local Alternatives to Global Agribusiness. *In the following viewpoint, which is adapted from their book, the authors argue that buying locally grown foods is the best way to support the global economy. Buying local decreases the amount of money spent on maintaining large storehouses of food and on the costs necessary to ship food to consumers far from where it is grown. In addition, Norberg-Hodge and Gorelick assert that governments should develop stronger global food trade regulations while decreasing regulations on the local food trade.*

As you read, consider the following questions:

1. As noted by the authors, what is global food?
2. How many farmers are in Europe's Common Agricultural Policy?
3. What is local food, as explained by the authors?

Today's mounting social and ecological crises demand responses that are broad, deep, and strategic. Given the widespread destruction wrought by globalisation, it seems

Helena Norberg-Hodge and Steven Gorelick, "Bringing the Food Economy Home," *The Ecologist*, September 2002. Reproduced by permission.

clear that the most powerful solutions will involve a fundamental change in direction—towards *localizing* rather than globalising economic activity. In fact, 'going local' may be the single most effective thing we can do.

Many people will find this claim exaggerated and unrealistic. But we have to ask ourselves whether it is realistic to continue pulling the entire global population into a single economy—one in which a small fraction of the population already uses the bulk of the world's resources. Today, roughly half the world's people, mostly in the South, still derive a large proportion of their needs from local economies. Do we really believe that those people's lives will be improved if we destroy these economies? What can globalisation offer the majority, other than unrealistic promises? Localisation would not only entail far less social and environmental upheaval, it would actually be far less costly to implement. In fact, every step towards the local, whether at the policy level or in our communities, would bring with it a whole cascade of benefits.

Rather than providing universal benefits, the global food system has been a major cause of hunger and environmental destruction around the world.

Localisation is essentially a process of decentralisation—shifting economic activity into the hands of millions of small- and medium-sized businesses instead of concentrating it in fewer and fewer mega-corporations. Localisation doesn't mean that every community would be entirely self-reliant; it simply means striking a balance between trade and local production by diversifying economic activity and shortening the distance between producers and consumers wherever possible.

Where should the first steps towards localisation take place? Since food is something everyone, everywhere, needs every day, a shift from global food to local food would have the greatest impact of all.

Social and Economic Costs of Global Food

Global food is based on an economic theory: Instead of producing a diverse range of food crops, every nation and region should specialise in one or two globally traded commodities—those they can produce cheaply enough to compete with every other producer. The proceeds from exporting those commodities are then used to buy food for local consumption. According to the theory, everyone will benefit.

The theory, as it turns out, is wrong. Rather than providing universal benefits, the global food system has been a major cause of hunger and environmental destruction around the world.

The environment has been hit particularly hard. The global system demands centralised collection of tremendous quantities of single crops, leading to the creation of huge monocultures. Monocultures, in turn, require massive inputs of pesticides, herbicides and chemical fertilisers. These practices systematically eliminate biodiversity from farmland, and lead to soil erosion, eutrophication [an increase of nutrients in a body of water that causes a speed up of plant growth and the eventual loss of animal life] of waterways, and the poisoning of surrounding ecosystems.

People are generally unaware that most of what they spend on food goes to corporate middlemen, not farmers.

Since global food is destined for distant markets, food miles have gone up astronomically, making food transport a major contributor to fossil fuel use, pollution, and greenhouse gas emissions. In the US [United States], for example, transporting food within the nation's borders accounts for over 20 percent of all commodity transport, and results in at least 120 million tonnes of CO_2 [carbon dioxide] emissions every year. In the UK [United Kingdom], imports of food and animal feed require over 83 billion tonne-kms [represents the transfer of one tonne over one kilometre] of transport, use 1.6 billion litres of fuel, and emit more than 4 million tonnes of CO_2. Much of this transport is utterly needless, since the 'logic' of global trade leads countries to simultaneously import and export the same commodity.

As farms have become larger and more mechanised, the number of farmers has steadily declined. The six founding countries of Europe's Common Agricultural Policy (CAP) had 22 million farmers in 1957; today that number has fallen to about 7 million. In the US, 6.8 million farms were in operation in 1935; today there are only one-fourth as many.

The global food system saps rural economies in other ways. People are generally unaware that most of what they spend on food goes to corporate middlemen, not farmers. In the US, for example, distributors, marketers, and input suppliers take 91 cents out of every food dollar, while farmers keep only 9 cents. As global corporations take over food marketing, small shopkeepers are also being squeezed out: In the 1990s alone, some 1,000 independent food shops—grocers, bakers, butchers and fishmongers—closed in the UK each year.

In the South, the globalisation of food is driving literally millions of farming families from the land. Dolma Tsering, a farmer in northern India, described what has happened in her village: "Whole families used to work on the land. We grew almost everything we needed. Now imported wheat is destroying our market. It's just not worth going to the trouble of producing food anymore, and the village is being emptied of people." Throughout the South, most of those displaced people will end up in urban slums—without community, without connection to the land, without a secure and healthy food supply.

The Declining Quality of Food

Because of the global food system, people around the world are induced to eat largely the same foods. In this way, farm

Local Versus Imported Ingredients: Iowa

One Iowa study found that the ingredients for a meal made from local sources traveled an average of 74 kilometers (45 miles) to reach their destination, compared with 2,577 kilometers (1,550 miles) if the same ingredients had been bought from the usual distant sources nationwide.

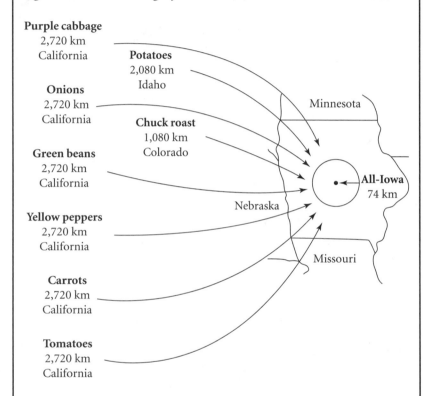

Purple cabbage
2,720 km
California

Potatoes
2,080 km
Idaho

Onions
2,720 km
California

Minnesota

Chuck roast
1,080 km
Colorado

Green beans
2,720 km
California

All-Iowa
74 km

Yellow peppers
2,720 km
California

Nebraska

Carrots
2,720 km
California

Missouri

Tomatoes
2,720 km
California

TAKEN FROM: Worldwatch Institute, "Globetrotting Food Will Travel Farther Than Ever This Thanksgiving," November 21, 2002. www.worldwatch.org.

monocultures go hand in hand with a spreading *human* monoculture, in which people's tastes and habits are homogenised—in part through advertising, which promotes foods suited to monocultural production, mechanised harvesting, long-distance transport and long-term storage.

New additives and processes—like UHT [ultra-high temperature processing] milk—are continually developed to extend storage time. For harried consumers, food corporations also provide 'convenience' foods that can be reheated quickly in a microwave, and even items like 'macaroni and cheese on a stick' which can be eaten with one hand. Nutritional content? We're told not to worry, since some of the nutrients destroyed in processing can supposedly be reinserted. Flavour? Hundreds of additives are on hand to mimic the taste and texture of real food. Food quality? With producers in a competitive race to the bottom, it's not surprising that food poisoning cases are steadily increasing, and new diseases like BSE [commonly referred to as mad cow disease] have appeared.

Decades of government support for global trade have concentrated wealth and power in ever larger corporations, which increasingly dominate every aspect of the global food supply—from seed and feed to everything on supermarket shelves. Today just two companies, Cargill and Archer Daniels Midland, control 70 to 80 percent of the world's grain trade. One agribusiness, Philip Morris, gets ten cents out of every American food dollar—more than earned by all US farmers combined.

Benefits of the Local

Awareness is steadily growing that global food is altogether too costly—socially, environmentally, even economically. People are beginning to seek out local food, and a whole movement is gaining ground.

But what, exactly, are 'local food systems'? If the highest expression of the global food system is a plastic-wrapped, highly processed slab of junk food that has been transported thousands of miles, the archetype product of a local food system is fresh food raised on nearby farms and sold at farmers' markets and in independent local shops.

Local food is, simply, food produced for local and regional consumption. For that reason, 'food miles' are relatively small, which greatly reduces fossil fuel use and pollution. There are other environmental benefits as well. While global markets demand monocultural production—which systematically eliminates all but the cash crop from the land—local markets give farmers an incentive to diversify, which creates many niches on the farm for wild plant and animal species to occupy. Moreover, diversified farms cannot accommodate the heavy machinery used in monocultures, thereby eliminating a major cause of soil erosion. Diversification also lends itself to organic methods, since crops are far less susceptible to pest infestations.

Local food systems have economic benefits, too, since most of the money spent on food goes to the farmer, not corporate middlemen. Juan Moreno, a farmer in the Andalucian region of Spain, told us, "When we used to sell our vegetables to supermarkets we got almost nothing for them. Now, through the local co-op, we're getting much more—three times as much for some vegetables."

Even food security would increase if people depended more on local foods.

Small diversified farms can help reinvigorate entire rural economies, since they employ far more people per acre than large monocultures. In the UK, farms under 100 acres provide five times more jobs per acre than those over 500 acres. Moreover, wages paid to farm workers benefit local economies and communities far more than money paid for heavy equipment and the fuel to run it: The latter is almost immediately siphoned off to equipment manufacturers and oil companies, while wages paid to workers are spent locally.

Food Quality

Local food is usually far fresher—and therefore more nutritious—than global food. It also needs fewer preservatives or other additives, and organic methods can eliminate pesticide residues. Farmers can grow varieties that are best suited to local climate and soils, allowing flavour and nutrition to take precedence over transportability, shelf life and the whims of global markets. Animal husbandry can be integrated with crop production, providing healthier, more humane conditions for animals and a non-chemical source of fertility.

Even food security would increase if people depended more on local foods. Instead of being concentrated in a handful of corporations, control over food would be dispersed and decentralised. And if countries in the South were encouraged to use their labour and their best agricultural land for local needs rather than growing luxury crops for northern markets, the rate of endemic hunger would diminish as well.

Nonetheless, even many of those who acknowledge its negative effects have been led to believe that the global food system is necessary because it produces more food and delivers it at a lower price. In reality, however, the global food system is neither more productive than local systems nor is it really cheaper. Studies carried out all over the world show that small-scale, diversified farms have a higher total output per unit of land than large-scale monocultures. In fact, if providing food for the world's hungry is the priority, then the shift towards local food systems should begin immediately, since they do a far better job of feeding people.

Global food is also very costly, though most of those costs do not show up in its supermarket price. Instead, a large portion of what we pay for global food comes out of our taxes—to fund research into pesticides and biotech, to subsidise the transport, communications and energy infrastructures the system requires, and to pay for the foreign aid that pulls third world economies into the destructive global system. We pay in other ways for the environmental costs of global food, which are degrading the planet our children will inherit.

When we buy local food, we can actually pay less because we are not paying for excessive transport, wasteful packaging, advertising, and chemical additives—only for fresh, healthy and nutritious food. Most of our food dollar isn't going to bloated corporate agribusinesses, but to nearby farmers and small shopkeepers, enabling them to charge less while still earning more than if they were tied to the global system.

How Do We Go Local?

Local food systems have immense advantages, but most policy makers—in the belief that more trade is always better—systematically support the further globalisation of food. As a result, identical products are crisscrossing the globe, with no other purpose than enriching the corporate middlemen that control the global food supply.

An immediate first step would be to press for policy changes to ensure that identical products are not being both imported and exported. If we eliminate needless trade in everything from wheat, milk and potatoes to apple juice and live animals, the reduction in transport alone would bring immediate benefits. What's more, if people around the world were allowed to eat their own bread and drink their own milk, giant corporations wouldn't profit every time we sit down to eat.

Such a step would require a rethinking of 'free trade' dogma. Trade treaties need to be rewritten, reestablishing the rights of citizens to protect their economies and resources from corporate predators.

At the same time, subsidies that now support the global food system need to be shifted towards more localised systems. Governments have spent tremendous sums of taxpayers' money to prop up a costly food system which pretends to provide 'cheap' food. If even a fraction of that sum were devoted to supporting local food systems instead, the cost of local food would decrease substantially, and its availability [would] rapidly grow.

Shifts in energy policy—which now heavily subsidise the large-scale centralised energy systems needed for global trade and industrial 'development' of all kinds—are critically important. In the South, where the energy infrastructure is still being built up, a shift towards a decentralised renewable energy path could be easily implemented, at a fraction of the cost in dollars and human upheaval that huge dams, nuclear power and fossil fuels entail.

Governments have spent tremendous sums of taxpayers' money to prop up a costly food system which pretends to provide 'cheap' food.

We also need to recognise the importance of local knowledge to maintain existing local food systems, and to reclaim those that have been largely lost. Today, a one-size-fits-all educational model is being imposed worldwide, eliminating much of the knowledge and skills people need to live on their own resources, in their own places on the earth.

Changes in tax policy would also help to promote food localisation. Now, tax credits for capital- and energy-intensive technologies favour the largest and most global producers. Meanwhile the more labour-intensive methods of small-scale diversified producers are penalised through income taxes, payroll taxes and other taxes on labour.

Reregulating Global Trade and Deregulating Local Trade

As we've seen, the steady deregulation of global trade and finance has led to the emergence of giant corporations whose activities are highly polluting and socially exploitative. This in turn has created a need for ever more social and environmental regulations, along with a massive bureaucracy to administer them. That bureaucracy is strangling smaller businesses with paperwork, inspections, fines, and the cost of mandated technologies. The regulatory burden is too great for the small to bear, while the big happily pay up and grow bigger as their smaller competitors die out. How many dairies have gone out of business because they had to have stainless steel sinks, when porcelain had served them well for generations?

Today, there is an urgent need to *re*regulate global trade, by allowing national and regional governments to control the activities of TNCs [transnational corporations]. At the same time, there is an equally urgent need to *de*regulate local trade, which by its nature is far less likely to damage human health and the environment.

These policy and regulatory shifts would open up space for thousands of community-based inititatives—many of them already under way—to flourish. From CSAs [community supported agriculture] and box schemes to farmers' markets, food co-ops, and buy-local campaigns, people have already begun the hands-on work needed to rebuild their local food systems. But these efforts will fall short if government policies continue to tilt the playing field towards the large and global.

Shortening the links between farmers and consumers may be one of the most strategic and enjoyable ways to bring about fundamental change for the better.

When government ministers blindly promote trade for the sake of trade while at the same time discussing reductions in CO_2 emissions, the possibility of sensible policy shifts can seem remote. And so it is, unless activists and other citizens unite behind the anti-global and pro-local banners, and exert powerful pressure from below. Already, unprecedented alliances have been created. Environmentalists and labour unionists, farmers and deep ecologists, people from North and

South—are all linking hands to say 'no' to an economic steam-roller that destroys jobs as quickly as it destroys species, that threatens the livelihood of farmers while driving up the price of healthy food in the marketplace.

Still more work is needed, however, including education campaigns to reveal the connections between our many crises, to spell out the truth about trade and the way we measure progress, and to graphically describe the ecological, social, psychological and economic benefits of localising and decentralising our economies.

Shortening the links between farmers and consumers may be one of the most strategic and enjoyable ways to bring about fundamental change for the better. How satisfying it is to know that by taking a step which is so good for us and our families, we are also making a very real contribution to preserving diversity, protecting jobs and rural livelihoods and the environment, all over the world.

Free Trade Has Created the Global Food Crisis

Walden Bello

Walden Bello is a fellow of the Transnational Institute and a professor of sociology at the University of the Philippines. In the following viewpoint, he argues that free trade has created a global crisis of food dependency. Countries such as Mexico, which used to lead the world in corn production, now depend on corn exports from the United States to feed their people. In essence, free trade partnerships have put the world's farmers out of business to make way for large agribusinesses that control the world's food supply. Without reform, Bello warns, world hunger will increase.

As you read, consider the following questions:

1. By how much did the price of tortillas increase in Mexico in 2007?
2. What percentage of the world's rice is traded?
3. What is VIA?

The global rise in food prices is not only a consequence of using food crops to produce biofuels, but of the "free trade" policies promoted by international financial institutions. Now peasant organizations are leading the opposition to a capitalist industrial agriculture.

When tens of thousands of people staged demonstrations in Mexico last year [2007] to protest a 60-percent increase in the price of tortillas, many analysts pointed to biofuel as the culprit. Because of US [United States] government subsidies, American farmers were devoting more and more acreage to corn for ethanol than for food, which sparked a steep rise in corn prices. The diversion of corn from tortillas to biofuel was certainly one cause of skyrocketing prices, though speculation on biofuel demand by transnational middlemen may have played a bigger role. However, an intriguing question escaped many observers: How on earth did Mexicans, who live in the land where corn was domesticated, become dependent on US imports in the first place?

Eroding Mexican Agriculture

The Mexican food crisis cannot be fully understood without taking into account the fact that in the years preceding the tortilla crisis, the homeland of corn had been converted to a corn-importing economy by "free market" policies promoted by the International Monetary Fund (IMF), the World Bank and Washington. The process began with the early 1980s debt crisis. One of the two largest developing-country debtors, Mexico was forced to beg for money from the [World] Bank and IMF to service its debt to international commercial banks. The quid pro quo for a multibillion-dollar bailout was what a member of the World Bank executive board described as "unprecedented thoroughgoing interventionism" designed to eliminate high tariffs, state regulations and government support institutions, which neoliberal doctrine identified as barriers to economic efficiency.

Interest payments rose from 19 percent of total government expenditures in 1982 to 57 percent in 1988, while capital expenditures dropped from an already low 19.3 percent to 4.4 percent. The contraction of government spending translated into the dismantling of state credit, government-subsidized agricultural inputs, price supports, state marketing boards and extension services. Unilateral liberalization of agricultural trade pushed by the IMF and World Bank also contributed to the destabilization of peasant producers.

This blow to peasant agriculture was followed by an even larger one in 1994, when the North American Free Trade Agreement [NAFTA] went into effect. Although NAFTA had a fifteen-year phaseout of tariff protection for agricultural products, including corn, highly subsidized US corn quickly flooded in, reducing prices by half and plunging the corn sector into chronic crisis. Largely as a result of this agreement, Mexico's status as a net food importer has now been firmly established.

With the shutting down of the state marketing agency for corn, distribution of US corn imports and Mexican grain has come to be monopolized by a few transnational traders, like US-owned Cargill and partly US-owned Maseca, operating on both sides of the border. This has given them tremendous power to speculate on trade trends, so that movements in bio-fuel demand can be manipulated and magnified many times over. At the same time, monopoly control of domestic trade has ensured that a rise in international corn prices does not translate into significantly higher prices paid to small producers.

It has become increasingly difficult for Mexican corn farmers to avoid the fate of many of their fellow corn cultivators and other smallholders in sectors such as rice, beef, poultry and pork, who have gone under because of the advantages conferred by NAFTA on subsidized US producers. According to a 2003 Carnegie Endowment [for International Peace] report, imports of US agricultural products threw at least 1.3 million farmers out of work—many of whom have since found their way to the United States.

Prospects are not good, since the Mexican government continues to be controlled by neoliberals who are systematically dismantling the peasant support system, a key legacy of the Mexican Revolution. As Food First[/Institute for Food and Development Policy] executive director Eric Holt-Giménez sees it, "It will take time and effort to recover smallholder capacity, and there does not appear to be any political will for this—to say nothing of the fact that NAFTA would have to be renegotiated."

The Philippines provides a grim example of how neoliberal economic restructuring transforms a country from a net food exporter to a net food importer.

Creating a Rice Crisis in the Philippines

That the global food crisis stems mainly from free market restructuring of agriculture is clearer in the case of rice. Unlike corn, less than 10 percent of world rice production is traded. Moreover, there has been no diversion of rice from food consumption to biofuels. Yet this year alone [2008], prices nearly tripled, from $380 a ton in January to more than $1,000 in April. Undoubtedly, the inflation stems partly from speculation by wholesaler cartels at a time of tightening supplies. However, as with Mexico and corn, the big puzzle is why a number of formerly self-sufficient rice-consuming countries have become severely dependent on imports.

The Philippines provides a grim example of how neoliberal economic restructuring transforms a country from a net food exporter to a net food importer. The Philippines is the world's largest importer of rice. Manila's desperate effort to secure supplies at any price has become front-page news, and pictures of soldiers providing security for rice distribution in poor communities have become emblematic of the global crisis.

The broad contours of the Philippines' story are similar to those of Mexico. Dictator Ferdinand Marcos was guilty of many crimes and misdeeds, including failure to follow through on land reform, but one thing he cannot be accused of is starving the agricultural sector of government funds. To head off peasant discontent, the regime provided farmers with subsidized fertilizer and seeds, launched credit schemes, and built rural infrastructure. During the 14 years of the dictatorship, it was only during one year, 1973, that rice had to be imported owing to widespread damage wrought by typhoons. When Marcos fled the country in 1986, there were reported to be 900,000 metric tons of rice in government warehouses.

Paradoxically, the next few years under the new democratic dispensation saw the gutting of government investment capacity. As in Mexico the World Bank and IMF, working on behalf of international creditors, pressured the Corazon Aquino administration to make repayment of the $26 billion foreign debt a priority. Aquino acquiesced, though she was warned by the country's top economists that the "search for a recovery program that is consistent with a debt repayment schedule determined by our creditors is a futile one."

Between 1986 and 1993 8 percent to 10 percent of GDP [gross domestic product] left the Philippines yearly in debt-service payments—roughly the same proportion as in Mexico. Interest payments as a percentage of expenditures rose from 7 percent in 1980 to 28 percent in 1994; capital expenditures plunged from 26 percent to 16 percent. In short, debt servicing became the national budgetary priority.

Spending on agriculture fell by more than half. The World Bank and its local acolytes [followers] were not worried, however, since one purpose of the belt-tightening was to get the private sector to energize the countryside. But agricultural capacity quickly eroded. Irrigation stagnated, and by the end of the 1990s only 17 percent of the Philippines' road network was paved, compared with 82 percent in Thailand and 75 percent in Malaysia. Crop yields were generally anemic, with the average rice yield in rice of 2.8 metric tons per hectare way below those in China, Vietnam and Thailand, where governments actively promoted rural production. The post-Marcos agrarian reform program shriveled, deprived of funding for support services, which had been the key to successful reforms in Taiwan and South Korea.

The consequences of the Philippines joining the [World Trade Organization] barreled through the rest of its agriculture like a super-typhoon.

A Cutback in Programs

As in Mexico, Filipino peasants were confronted with full-scale retreat of the state as provider of comprehensive support—a role they had come to depend on.

And the cutback in agricultural programs was followed by trade liberalization, with the Philippines' 1995 entry into the World Trade Organization [WTO] having the same effect as Mexico's joining NAFTA. WTO membership required the Philippines to eliminate quotas on all agricultural imports except rice and allow a certain amount of each commodity to enter at low tariff rates. While the country was allowed to maintain a quota on rice imports, it nevertheless had to admit the equivalent of 1 to 4 percent of domestic consumption over the next ten years. In fact, because of gravely weakened production resulting from lack of state support, the government imported much more than that to make up for possible shortfalls. These imports, which rose from 263,000 metric tons in 1995 to 2.1 million tons in 1998, depressed the price of rice, discouraging farmers and keeping growth in production at a rate far below that of the country's two top suppliers, Thailand and Vietnam.

The consequences of the Philippines joining the WTO barreled through the rest of its agriculture like a super-typhoon. Swamped by cheap corn imports—much of it subsidized US grain—farmers reduced land devoted to corn from 3.1 million hectares in 1993 to 2.5 million in 2000. Massive importation of chicken parts nearly killed that industry, while surges in imports destabilized the poultry, hog and vegetable industries.

During the 1994 campaign to ratify WTO membership, government economists, coached by their World Bank handlers, promised that losses in corn and other traditional crops would be more than compensated for by the new export industry of "high value-added" crops like cut flowers, asparagus and broccoli. Little of this materialized. Nor did many of the 500,000 agricultural jobs that were supposed to be created yearly by the magic of the market; instead, agricultural employment dropped from 11.2 million in 1994 to 10.8 million in 2001.

The one-two punch of IMF-imposed adjustment and WTO-imposed trade liberalization swiftly transformed a largely self-sufficient agricultural economy into an import-dependent one as it steadily marginalized farmers. It was a wrenching process, the pain of which was captured by a Filipino government negotiator during a WTO session in Geneva. "Our small producers," he said, "are being slaughtered by the gross unfairness of the international trading environment."

The Great Transformation

The experience of Mexico and the Philippines was paralleled in one country after another subjected to the ministrations of the IMF and the WTO. A study of fourteen countries by the UN's [United Nations'] Food and Agricultural Organization found that the levels of food imports in 1995–98 exceeded those in 1990–94. This was not surprising, since one of the main goals of the WTO's Agreement on Agriculture was to open up markets in developing countries so they could absorb surplus production in the North. As then US Agriculture Secretary John Block put it in 1986, "The idea that developing

Barry Deutsch, "Free Trade: Freedom to Do as U.S. Corporations Demand," October 9, 2008. Copyright © Barry Deutsch, leftycartoons.com.

countries should feed themselves is an anachronism from a bygone era. They could better ensure their food security by relying on US agricultural products, which are available in most cases at lower cost."

There is little room for the hundreds of millions of rural and urban poor in this integrated global market.

What Block did not say was that the lower cost of US products stemmed from subsidies, which became more massive with each passing year despite the fact that the WTO was supposed to phase them out. From $367 billion in 1995, the total amount of agricultural subsidies provided by developed-country governments rose to $388 billion in 2004. Since the late 1990s subsidies have accounted for 40 percent of the value of agricultural production in the European Union and 25 percent in the United States.

The apostles of the free market and the defenders of dumping may seem to be at different ends of the spectrum, but the policies they advocate are bringing about the same result: a globalized capitalist industrial agriculture. Developing countries are being integrated into a system where export-oriented production of meat and grain is dominated by large industrial farms like those run by the Thai multinational CP [Charoen Pokphand Group] and where technology is continually upgraded by advances in genetic engineering from firms like Monsanto. And the elimination of tariff and nontariff barriers is facilitating a global agricultural supermarket of elite and middle-class consumers serviced by grain-trading corporations like Cargill and Archer Daniels Midland and transnational food retailers like the British-owned Tesco and the French-owned Carrefour.

There is little room for the hundreds of millions of rural and urban poor in this integrated global market. They are confined to giant suburban favelas [shantytowns], where they contend with food prices that are often much higher than the supermarket prices, or to rural reservations, where they are trapped in marginal agricultural activities and increasingly vulnerable to hunger. Indeed, within the same country, famine in the marginalized sector sometimes coexists with prosperity in the globalized sector.

This is not simply the erosion of national food self-sufficiency or food security, but what Africanist Deborah Bryceson of Oxford calls "de-peasantization"—the phasing out of a mode of production to make the countryside a more congenial site for intensive capital accumulation. This transformation is a traumatic one for hundreds of millions of people, since peasant production is not simply an economic activity. It is an ancient way of life, a culture, which is one reason displaced or marginalized peasants in India have taken to committing suicide. In the state of Andhra Pradesh, farmer suicides rose from 233 in 1998 to 2,600 in 2002; in Maharashtra, suicides more than tripled, from 1,083 in 1995 to 3,926 in 2005. One estimate is that some 150,000 Indian farmers have taken their lives. Collapse of prices from trade liberalization and loss of control over seeds to biotech firms is part of a comprehensive problem, says global justice activist Vandana Shiva: "Under globalization, the farmer is losing her/his social, cultural, economic identity as a producer. A farmer is now a 'consumer' of costly seeds and costly chemicals sold by powerful global corporations through powerful landlords and money lenders locally." . . .

"A farmer is now a 'consumer' of costly seeds and costly chemicals sold by powerful global corporations."

Food Sovereignty: An Alternative Paradigm?

It is not only defiance from governments . . . and dissent from their erstwhile allies that are undermining the IMF and the World Bank. Peasant organizations around the world have become increasingly militant in their resistance to the globalization of industrial agriculture. Indeed, it is because of pressure from farmers' groups that the governments of the South have refused to grant wider access to their agricultural markets and demanded a massive slashing of US and EU [European Union] agricultural subsidies, which brought the WTO's Doha [Development] Round of negotiations to a standstill.

Farmers' groups have networked internationally; one of the most dynamic to emerge is Via Campesina (Peasant's Path). Via not only seeks to get "WTO out of agriculture" and opposes the paradigm of a globalized capitalist industrial agriculture, it also proposes an alternative-food sovereignty. Food sovereignty means, first of all, the right of a country to determine its production and consumption of food and the exemption of agriculture from global trade regimes like that of the WTO. It also means consolidation of a smallholder-centered agriculture via protection of the domestic market from low-priced imports; remunerative prices for farmers and fisherfolk; abolition of all direct and indirect export subsidies; and the phasing out of domestic subsidies that promote unsustainable agriculture. Via's platform also calls for an end to the Trade-Related [Aspects of] Intellectual Property Rights regime, or TRIPs, which allows corporations to patent plant seeds; opposes agro-technology based on genetic engineering; and demands land reform. In contrast to an integrated global monoculture, Via offers the vision of an international agricultural economy composed of diverse national agricultural economies trading with one another but focused primarily on domestic production.

Food sovereignty means . . . the right of a country to determine its production and consumption of food and the exemption of agriculture from global trade regimes.

Once regarded as relics of the pre-industrial era, peasants are now leading the opposition to a capitalist industrial agriculture that would consign them to the dustbin of history. They have become what Karl Marx described as a politically conscious "class for itself," contradicting his predictions about their demise. With the global food crisis, they are moving to center stage—and they have allies and supporters. For as peasants refuse to go gently into that good night and fight de-peasantization, developments in the twenty-first century are revealing the panacea of globalized capitalist industrial agriculture to be a nightmare. With environmental crises multiplying, the social dysfunctions of urban-industrial life piling up and industrialized agriculture creating greater food insecurity, the farmers' movement increasingly has relevance not only to peasants, but to everyone threatened by the catastrophic consequences of global capital's vision for organizing production, community and life itself.

The Fair Trade Coffee Movement Can Do More to Help International Farmers

Jeremy Weber

Jeremy Weber is a graduate student in the Department of Agricultural and Applied Economics at the University of Wisconsin-Madison. *In the following viewpoint, he argues that Fair Trade coffee, or coffee that has been certified by the Fairtrade Labelling Organizations International (FLO), does not help small coffee growers. Although Fair Trade coffee is marketed as a way to support coffee farmers and pickers across the globe, Weber asserts that purchasing Fair Trade coffee simply further supports the largest coffee companies. Participation in the Fair Trade market is costly and is often limited to well-established companies, he says.*

As you read, consider the following questions:

1. As cited by the author, how much is Fair Trade coffee per pound?

2. What percent of Fair Trade coffee sold in the United States is organic, according to the viewpoint?

3. Who is the largest purchaser of Fair Trade coffee in North America, according to Weber?

Jeremy Weber, "Fair Trade Coffee Enthusiasts Should Confront Reality," *CATO Journal*, vol. 27, no. 1, Winter 2007, pp. 109–117. Copyright © 2007 by Cato Institute. Republished with permission of Cato Institute, conveyed through Copyright Clearance Center, Inc.

From university cafeterias to supermarkets in the developed world, people are buying Fair Trade (FT) coffee certified by the FLO-Cert, the certifying entity of Fairtrade Labelling Organizations International (FLO). The assumption is that such purchases will contribute to the welfare of marginalized producers in the developing world. While sales of FT coffee in Europe have stabilized, the North American and Japanese markets are growing rapidly. Total sales increased 40 percent from 2004 to 2005, to a total volume of 33,992 metric tons (MT) (FTO 2005).

What is "Fair Trade"? According to FINE, the umbrella organization that comprises the four largest Fair Trade organizations (FLO, International Federation for Alternative Trade, Network of European Worldshops, and the European Fair Trade Association),

> Fair Trade is a trading partnership, based on dialogue, transparency and respect, that seeks greater equity in international trade. It contributes to sustainable development by offering better trading conditions to, and securing the rights of, marginalized producers and workers—especially in the South [FINE 2001].

The FINE definition optimistically assumes that the trading partnerships and conditions promoted by Fair Trade necessarily "contribute to sustainable development." It is true that the Fair Trade coffee system—the producers, exporters, importers, and retailers operating by the rules and standards of FLO—has improved living standards for many participating coffee growers (Bacon 2005, Raynolds 2004). Yet the system faces vexing issues such as a disconnect between promotional materials and reality, excess supply, and the marginalization of economically disadvantaged producers and groups. Those in-

Jeremy Weber is a graduate student in the Agricultural and Applied Economics Department at the University of Wisconsin-Madison. He spent 10 months in Peru researching Fair Trade coffee and working with coffee producer organizations with the support of a Fullbright grant.

volved in Fair Trade coffee debates and governance must address these issues if Fair Trade is to be an effective mechanism for rural development in coffee producing regions.

The Search for Culprits

Unfortunately, many of those close to the movement prefer to blame profit-seeking corporations for hijacking Fair Trade instead of objectively analyzing the workings of the Fair Trade coffee system. For example, the financial manager of a Peruvian Fair Trade coffee exporter explained to me that his company's critique of FLO is that it will allow companies like Nestlé to participate, even though such companies are only in Fair Trade for the profit. Never mind that the company he works for is a privately owned, for-profit export company. As Adam Smith so well noted, the interest of the merchants (including coffee exporters) is always to narrow the competition and expand the market. Likewise, the executive director of a major retailer of Fair Trade coffee assured me that the problem with Fair Trade is the participation of too many ideologically uncommitted entities. Even though this director was new to the job and had never visited a Fair Trade coffee cooperative, he had already determined the cause of the problem. This knee-jerk, blame-greedy-corporations reaction is common among Fair Trade enthusiasts. At the 2nd International Fair Trade Colloquium held in Montreal in June of 2006 the hot topic was the participation of large corporations in the Fair Trade coffee system (Nebenzahl 2006).

The Gap: Promotional Materials and Reality

While the participation of large transnational companies may alter the dynamics of the Fair Trade coffee system, Fair Trade faces more serious practical issues. A large gap divides the story depicted by Fair Trade marketing materials from the standards of FLO and the advantages of producer participation. This misleading representation of Fair Trade has led many socially conscious coffee drinkers to hold unexamined assumptions about the benefits of Fair Trade.

Many Fair Trade coffee drinkers also believe that hired laborers on a Fair Trade certified coffee farm receive minimum wage of some sort.

In trying to boost sales many retailers claim that Fair Trade coffee guarantees a living wage to coffee growers. A major promoter of Fair Trade coffee, Global Exchange (2005), states on its Web site, "Fair Trade guarantees to poor farmers organized in cooperatives around the world: a living wage." While it remains to be seen what constitutes a "living wage," in reality, Fair Trade guarantees nothing to producers. Fair Trade ensures a minimum price to *organizations* of producers, but not to individual producers. The organization serves as an intermediary between the producer and the market. Producers receive the price stipulated in the organization's export contract, which must meet or exceed the Fair Trade minimum price, minus the expenses of the organization. Since Fair Trade eliminates "unnecessary" intermediaries, producer organizations must perform the tasks previously conducted by those intermediaries. In this arrangement, an organization must obtain financing to buy coffee from its members, sort and process coffee, and coordinate export logistics. Each of those activities generates expenses, which if not managed effectively and efficiently, can consume much of the higher Fair Trade price before it reaches growers. In some cases, organizations' export costs have been high enough to induce member producers to sell to the local market instead of to their organization for the Fair Trade market.[1]

1. This situation is exacerbated as the price in the conventional coffee market rises. Higher costs associated with Fair Trade coffee require that the Fair Trade price maintain a significant margin above the conventional price. If the conventional price rises above the Fair Trade minimum price, according to Fair Trade rules the importer must offer the supplying organization at least the market price plus five cents per pound.

Many Fair Trade coffee drinkers also believe that hired laborers on a Fair Trade certified coffee farm receive a minimum wage of some sort. In the case of coffee sold by producer organizations, wage standards only apply to employees of the organization. Specific standards regarding temporary workers hired by coffee farmers do not exist. Most hired labor on small-scale coffee farms, however, is seasonal. Standards for small farmers' organizations state, "Where workers are casually hired by farmers themselves, the organizations should take steps to improve working conditions and to ensure that such workers share the benefits of Fair Trade" (FLO 2005). Hal Weitzman of the *Financial Times* visited five Fair Trade farms in northern Peru and found that four of the farms paid workers below the Peruvian minimum wage (Weitzman 2006).

Such payments do not violate Fair Trade standards. In its response to the Weitzman article, the Fairtrade Foundation reiterated its norms regarding workers hired by small-scale producers and recognized "that the members of these producer organisations are small farmers who struggle to earn a decent livelihood for themselves and their families" (The Fairtrade Foundation 2006). Unfortunately, Fair Trade promotional materials have lured coffee drinkers into believing that Fair Trade guarantees farmers and workers a fair or living wage, which most consumers probably interpret to mean a wage at or above the legal minimum in the coffee-producing country.

The imbalance between the supply of Fair Trade certified coffee and consumer demand has existed for at least 10 years.

Trying to Strong-Arm the Market

Another pressing matter that has received little attention in Fair Trade circles concerns primary and secondary effects of the Fair Trade movement's attempt to strong-arm the market by establishing a minimum price of $1.24 per pound.[2] A price floor is created if the world coffee market price is less than $1.24. As anyone who has taken basic economics would predict, a minimum price set above the market price will act as a price floor, leading to excess supply. This has been the case in the Fair Trade coffee market. The above-market price, however, does little to increase coffee production as suggested recently in the *Economist* (2006). Most Fair Trade certified producers sell a fraction of their coffee to the Fair Trade market and the rest to the conventional market. FLO increases the supply of Fair Trade coffee by certifying additional producer organizations and channeling existing production into the Fair Trade market, not by inducing farmers to grow more coffee.

The imbalance between the supply of Fair Trade certified coffee and consumer demand has existed for at least 10 years. Bob Thomson, the former director of Fair TradeMark Canada, affirmed in 1995 that Fair Trade producers had a productive capacity of 250,000 MT of coffee for a demand of only 11,000 MT (Thomson 1995). In other words, the market only purchased around 13 percent of the production of certified coffee producers' organizations.[3] The imbalance between supply and demand was significant enough to cause FLO to temporarily close their registry to new members in 2002 (Vizcarra 2002). FLO estimated that the supply of Fair Trade certified coffee in Latin America, Asia, and Africa in 2002 was seven times greater than the quantity exported through Fair Trade channels (Murray, Raynolds, Taylor 2003).

---

2. This price includes the five cents per pound social premium given by Fair Trade and refers to Arabica-washed conventional coffee from South America.
3. In most industries, capacity does not equal production. In the Fair Trade system, however, most certified organizations only sell a fraction of what they produce to the Fair Trade market even though all of their coffee is technically Fair Trade certified. In other words, excess capacity refers to Fair Trade certified coffee being sold in the conventional market as opposed to an unharvested crop or fallow land.

The experience of the Peruvian coffee producer association, the Association of Ecological Producers (APROECO), confirms this reality. When APROECO applied for certification in 2001, FLO told the association that it already had 280 pending applications, but that it could prioritize APROECO's application if the association had a buyer.[4] Because the global coffee market suffered a profound crisis in the beginning of this decade, it is not surprising that there were 280 applications before that of APROECO. At the end of 2000, coffee prices dropped from about $1.10 per pound to $0.65 per pound. Prices only began to rise in 2004.

The increased difficulty of entering the Fair Trade market threatens to exclude the marginalized coffee growers who Fair Trade supposedly supports.

Figure 1 depicts the Fair Trade minimum price and the conventional market price during the coffee crises. The large gap between the Fair Trade price and the conventional price represents the incentive to obtain the FLO certification and sell to the Fair Trade market. Of course, if there were a free market, new entrants would increase supply and decrease price. The minimum price of $1.24 per pound, by definition, prevents that outcome. The problem with an excess supply of certified coffee is not that large quantities of coffee are dumped on world markets. Rather, the problem is that an excess supply results in increased barriers to entry and increased competition among producer organizations for a limited number of Fair Trade contracts. In particular, the increased difficulty of entering the Fair Trade market threatens to exclude the marginalized coffee growers who Fair Trade supposedly supports.

4. Interview with Orlando Diaz, 9/10/2005. As a manager of the coffee export company Pronatur, Diaz coordinated the certification processes for APROECO.

With an excess supply of coffee, the Fair Trade market has increasingly demanded organic coffee. The dual certification of Fair Trade and organic has allowed coffee organizations to differentiate their coffee in a saturated market. Between 1996 and 2000, exports of dual certified coffee (Fair Trade and organic) grew from 86.25 MT to 5,096 MT, an increase of about 5,800 percent (Raynolds 2002). According to Fair Trade fast facts, approximately 85 percent of Fair Trade coffee sold in the United States is certified organic (TransFair USA 2006).[5]

Quality standards have risen significantly since 2000. Furthermore, beginning in 2004 FLO began charging producer organizations $3,200 to become certified.[6] These increasing demands are easily understood when viewed in a market context of excess supply. In other words, barriers to entering the Fair Trade market have intensified to equilibrate supply and demand in a market with a price floor.

Most organizations need around $15,000 in financing to export one container of Fair Trade coffee.

Entry barriers affect who participates in the market. Entering the Fair Trade coffee market, especially the Fair Trade organic market, presents major difficulties for young producer organizations. Without assistance from development organizations or export companies, the very organizations and producers that Fair Trade targets have little chance of participating in the market. Obtaining the certification of the FLO requires someone within the organization to coordinate the involved certification process. The soliciting organization must also obtain an export contract and the necessary financing to buy and export coffee. Most organizations need around

5. TransFair USA is a member of FLO and is the only organization that audits Fair Trade transactions in the United States.
6. This fee varies depending on the size and nature of the organization being certified. The current fee listed by TransFair USA is €2,000 for a first-level organization of less than 500 producers.

$15,000 in financing to export one container of Fair Trade coffee. That short-term financing is needed to complement the pre-financing offered by the Fair Trade importer. (The FLO requires Fair Trade importers to provide a minimum pre-financing of 60 percent of the value of the export contract.) In addition, the organization needs $3,200 to pay FLO for its certification (Weber 2006).

The ideal of the Fair Trade movement is the participation of entities whose business is 100 percent Fair Trade certified. In reality, Starbucks is the largest purchaser of Fair Trade coffee in North America although Fair Trade coffee only comprises 3.7 percent of the company's purchases.

Since the Fair Trade coffee market is consistently demanding more and more organic coffee, many organizations find that they must become organic certified to obtain export contracts. The organic certification process is more expensive and demanding than that of FLO. Most organic certification programs last three years. Each year requires an external inspection from the certifying entity. An external inspection for an organization of 100 producers can generally cost around $2,000. The more significant cost, however, is in providing technical assistance in organic production norms to participating farmers. The total cost of implementing an organic certification program in four Peruvian coffee organizations ranged from $300 to more than $1,000 per producer (Weber 2006).

Increased barriers to entry have made it increasingly difficult for marginalized producers, which Fair Trade supposedly targets, to participate. As in most industries, increasing barriers to entry benefits those already established in the market. Such is the case in the Fair Trade coffee market, which is dominated primarily by those privileged groups who entered

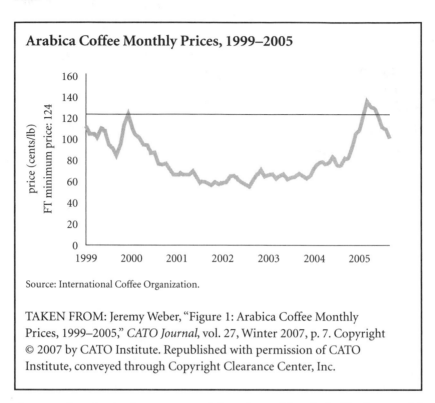

Arabica Coffee Monthly Prices, 1999–2005

price (cents/lb)
FT minimum price: 124

Source: International Coffee Organization.

TAKEN FROM: Jeremy Weber, "Figure 1: Arabica Coffee Monthly Prices, 1999–2005," *CATO Journal*, vol. 27, Winter 2007, p. 7. Copyright © 2007 by CATO Institute. Republished with permission of CATO Institute, conveyed through Copyright Clearance Center, Inc.

the market in its less competitive days. The Fair Trade model based on a minimum price will inevitably produce a tension between concentrating market shares to a few groups, which leaves many out of the Fair Trade system, and distributing market shares to many groups, which results in each producer selling only a fraction of his production to the Fair Trade market.

Where to Go from Here? Get Comfortable with the Market

A troubling gap lies between the purported benefits of Fair Trade and reality. Nevertheless, participation in Fair Trade networks has undoubtedly generated benefits for many producers. Integrating new producer groups into Fair Trade, however, depends on the size of the market. Ironically, the most obvious way to increase coffee sales, enlisting the resources of mainstream coffee retailers, is seen by many enthusiasts as the biggest threat facing Fair Trade. The ideal of the Fair Trade movement is the participation of entities whose business is 100 percent Fair Trade certified. In reality, Starbucks is the largest purchaser of Fair Trade coffee in North America although Fair Trade coffee only comprises 3.7 percent of the company's purchases.[7]

Sue Mecklenburg, the vice president of sustainable procurement for Starbucks, believes that a pressing question is, "Can Fair Trade get comfortable in the competitive market?" The size of the Fair Trade coffee market and the competitiveness of the entities that link producers to the market affect Fair Trade's ability to generate benefits for producers. As stated previously, poor management of the export process by producer organizations can consume much of the higher Fair Trade price before it reaches growers. Some producer organizations such as APROECO in Peru have entered partnerships with companies to capitalize on the scale and expertise of private export companies. APROECO's relationship with a private export company also allowed the organization to overcome the entry barriers of the Fair Trade and organic markets (e.g., certification and contractual costs). A study of Costa Rican coffee mills by Loraine Ronchi of the World Bank suggests that such partnerships may increase prices paid to farmers. The study found that Fair Trade cooperative mills had lower price markdowns (defined as the difference between the price paid to mills and the price that mills paid to coffee farmers) than non-Fair Trade, non-foreign owned mills. At the same time, vertically integrated multinational mills had a similar effect of lowering price markdowns when compared with non-foreign owned mills (Ronchi 2006). FLO should welcome partnerships between producer organizations and private companies instead of insisting that producer organiza-

7. Interview with Sue Mecklenburg, September 11, 2006.

tions assume all export responsibilities. Social justice goals and efficiency can complement each other.

If Fair Trade is dominated by those who see mainstream for-profit companies as intrinsically destructive, the movement will remain a fringe, niche market that supports a few privileged groups. Fair Trade enthusiasts must spend more time asking hard, practical questions about how Fair Trade functions and less time searching for enemies. Only with a strong dose of practicality and self-critique can the Fair Trade movement create an effective mechanism for promoting development in coffee-producing communities.

References

Bacon, C. (2005) "Confronting the Coffee Crisis: Can Fair Trade, Organic, and Specialty Coffees Reduce Small-Scale Farmer Vulnerability in Northern Nicaragua?" *World Development* 33 (3): 497–511.

The Economist (2006) "Voting with Your Trolley: Food Politics." (9 December).

The Fairtrade Foundation (2006) "Fairtrade Foundation Response to *Financial Times* Article" (11 September). Available at www.fairtrade.org.uk/pr110906.htm.

Fairtrade Labelling Organizations International (FLO) (2005) "Delivering Opportunities: Annual Report, 2005, 2006." Available at www.fairtrade.net/uploads/media/ FLO_Annual_Report_05.pdf.

FINE (2001) "Fair Trade Definition and Principles as agreed by FINE in December 2001." Available at www.eFair Trade aFair Trade.org/pdf/Fair-TDAP.pdf.

Global Exchange (2005) "What Is Fair Trade Coffee All About?" Available at ww.globalexchange.org/campaigns/ fairtrade/coffee/background.html.

Murray, D.; Raynolds, L.T.; and Taylor, P.L. (2003) "One Cup at a Time: Fair Trade and Poverty Alleviation in Latin America." Available at www.colostate.edu/Depts/Sociology/ Fair TradeResearchGroup.

———— (2004) "Building Producer Capacity via Global Networks." *Journal of International Development* 16 (8): 1109–21.

Nebenzahl, D. (2006) "Corporate Big Boys Smell the Coffee." *The Gazette* (16 June).

Raynolds, L.T. (2002) "Poverty Alleviation through the Participation in Fair Trade Networks: Existing Research and Critical Issues." Available at www.colostate.edu/Depts/Sociology/Fair TradeResearchGroup.

Ronchi, L. (2006) "'Fairtrade' and Market Failures in Agricultural Commodity Markets." World Bank Policy Research Working Paper No. 4011(September). Available at http://econ.worldbank.org.

Thomson, B. (1995) "Lessons Learned: Fair Trade and CED." Paper presented at the conference "Community Enterprise Development and Globalization" (November). Available at www.globalexchange.org/campaigns/fairtrade/coffee/coffeeBib.html.

TransFair USA (2006) "Fast Facts: Fair Trade Certified Specialty Coffee." Available at www.transfairusa.org/pdfs/fastfacts_coffee.pdf.

Vizcarra, G.K. (2002) "El Comercio Justo: Una Alternativa para la Agroindustria Rural en América Latina." Organización de las Naciones Unidas para la Agricultura y la Alimentación, Oficina Regional para América Latina y el Caribe (January). Available at www.rlc.fao.org/prior/desrural/agroindustria/pdf/comerjus.pdf.

Weber, J. (2006) "Rationing in the Fair Trade Coffee Market: Who Enters and How?" Paper presented at "The Second International Colloquium: Fair Trade and Sustainable Development," University of Quebec, Montreal, June 19–21.

Weitzman, H. (2006) "The Bitter Cost of 'Fair Trade' Coffee." *Financial Times* (8 September).

The Failing World Economy Will Continue to Challenge Egypt's Food Supply

David M. Malone

David M. Malone is president of Canada's International Development Research Centre, which provides financial support for scientific research. In the following viewpoint, Malone argues that Egypt's food supply will remain in jeopardy as long as the world's economy remains in fluctuation. He asserts that as global grain stocks go down, some commodity prices will continue to rise. In addition, Malone insists that following examples set forth by India and China might help Egypt alleviate some of its current agricultural struggles.

As you read, consider the following questions:

1. According to Malone, by how much has the price of rice increased over the past few years?
2. How much wheat does Egypt import, as cited in the viewpoint?
3. According to the author, what are three strategies that can be used to improve Egypt's agricultural situation?

A mong the reasons for the crisis in global food supply and prices is the fact that global grain stocks have been dropping for years. Meanwhile, prices of some commodities have

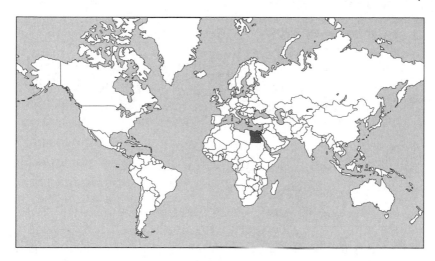

been rising progressively. The price of rice, for instance, quadrupled over previous years. Global demographics have increased pressure on both stocks and prices. Further, welcome economic success in much of the developing world, including Egypt, has altered eating habits. The stampede into biofuels in the West, in order to supplement finite oil and gas supplies, also handicapped food production.

Agricultural productivity and food security are complex challenges, not least because they relate intimately to issues such as water management, soil degradation and regeneration, climate change, the consumption preferences of the growing global middle class, and international trade arrangements. And in spite of terrible famines in Africa and the threat of hunger elsewhere, agriculture has largely fallen off the map of global concerns since the early 1980s.

Different Approaches to Agricultural Development

But decreased global investment in agricultural research and development over the past two decades can be reversed. Bad policies, adopted in panic or ignorance, can be stopped. Export embargoes and increased export taxes reassure in the short term, but create distortions worldwide and undermine access for the poorest countries and consumers.

India and China provide examples of what happens when different approaches to agricultural development are applied. On one hand, India's key economic reforms of the early 1990s centred on liberalisation favouring the manufacturing and services sectors. These were tremendously successful, but little was done for agriculture. China, on the other hand, starting its key reforms earlier, focused first on agriculture.

China's approach was to raise agricultural production by encouraging multiple experiments at the local level—simply put, it learned by doing. Only after it was clear what worked did Beijing launch a nationwide reform process that succeeded dramatically in raising production and decisively reducing rural poverty.

India was once at the apex of international achievement in agricultural innovation. Drawing on a wide variety of international grain types, pioneers of high-yielding hybrid seeds were able to achieve in the 1960s and 1970s a real "green revolution", boosting agricultural productivity at an impressive scale and making the country fully self-sufficient in its main food requirements for the first time in modern history. Scientific innovation was supported by energetic government policy. But then, as so often after success, attention and focus faded.

India remains, in good years, capable of meeting its main needs and simultaneously of earning sizeable sums from agricultural exports. Rather, it is the combination of Indian demographics with the growing success of the country's overall economy and environmental stress that demand attention. Increasingly prosperous Indians will be eating more—and probably wasting more also, as do middle classes everywhere.

Egypt has been quite successful in expanding its agricultural production in recent years. Thirty years ago, Egypt imported roughly 70 per cent of its wheat. Today, it normally imports only around 45 per cent. But precisely because the

"Forget the flat screen, Phil. I just found a sack of Basmati rice!" cartoon by Shelley Matheis, www.CartoonStock.com. Copyright © Shelley Matheis. Reproduction rights obtainable from CartoonStock.com.

Egyptian economy also has been performing better in recent years—hitting a growth rate in 2007–2008 of 7.2 per cent, not so far behind India's much admired 9.2 per cent—food consumption patterns have also been changing. Increasingly the middle class consumes meat, which requires a high input of grain and the import of much "red" meat.

The Limitations of Land Use

Egypt has performed well in reclaiming desert lands for large-scale agriculture that is economically more viable than the excessively sub-divided family plots in the Nile Valley and Delta could ever be. But there is a limit to how much more land can be reclaimed for agricultural purposes without better water management schemes. In spite of much effort, irrigation remains inefficient in much of Egypt's agriculture.

Further, in the Nile Valley and Delta, there is an urgent need to provide residents with better non-farm livelihoods that will induce people to stay in rural areas, knowing that they can derive a good living from higher-paying activities such as food processing.

[Egypt's] subsidy system, an important one for the poor, is wildly dysfunctional.

In this regard, in an insightful strategy for sustainable agricultural development through the year 2030, the Agricultural Research and Development Council of Egypt argues that Egyptian agricultural production needs to move up the value chain. A good start has been made in horticulture, with large markets normally available to Egypt in Europe and in the Gulf, although European demand for cut flowers may diminish significantly during the current economic downturn. But Egypt can do more and better in the lucrative areas of fruit and vegetables.

Egypt worries about self-sufficiency in food, as do many other nations. And yet its subsidy system, an important one for the poor, is wildly dysfunctional, with the rich also benefiting from subsidies, and much of the subsidised bread thought to be consumed by livestock rather than people. The system needs to be better targeted, squarely at poor communities.

Many developing countries, including Egypt, offer admirable human capital: optimistic, hard working, and, given a chance, entrepreneurial. But fulfilling their agricultural potential will require sound government policies, determined implementation and greater attention to more sustainable growth of farm produce. If the economic crisis gripping the world distracts attention from medium- and long-term challenges, such as agricultural productivity growth, its damage will be compounded well into the future.

Periodical Bibliography

The following articles have been selected to supplement the diverse views presented in this chapter.

Tom Arup	"Minister Calls for Free Trade Pact for Food," *Sydney Morning Herald* (Australia), November 30, 2009.
Tom Arup	"'Only Free Trade' Will End Hunger," *The Age* (Melbourne, Australia), November 29, 2009.
Ferghal Blaney	"Irish Prices Up by 40pc as a Global Food Crunch Bites Deeply," *Daily Mail* (UK), April 15, 2008.
Robert Knox	"Fair Trade Importer Says It's Ripe for Success," *Boston Globe*, January 4, 2010.
Hamish McDonald	"Food on India's Mind as Free-Trade Discussions Start," *Sydney Morning Herald* (Australia), May 20, 2008.
Daniele Pisanello	"What Do Food Safety and Fair Trade Stand for? Reconciling the Twofold Objective of EU Food Law," *European Food and Feed Law*, May 2009.
Reuters UK	"Biofuels Blamed for Food Costs," July 4, 2008. http://uk.reuters.com.
Harry Wallop	"Shoppers to 'Abandon Organic Foods to Cut Bills,'" *Daily Telegraph* (UK), May 20, 2008.

For Further Discussion

Chapter 1

1. Oliver Cann insists that global food safety standards need to be developed and implemented. Do you agree? If so, who should create and monitor these standards?

2. The remaining authors in this chapter argue that the world food supply, especially in certain countries, is in danger. Do you agree or disagree? Use examples from the viewpoints to explain your answer.

Chapter 2

1. The authors in this chapter offer a number of reasons for the world food shortage. Which arguments are most convincing? Explain your answer.

Chapter 3

1. Charles Benbrook, Donald R. Davis, and Preston K. Andrews argue that foods grown organically are healthier than foods grown with pesticides and other chemicals. On the other hand, Alan D. Dangour and his colleagues argue that organic food is not much different from foods grown conventionally. Based upon these arguments, do you think organic foods are beneficial to humans?

2. Chris Brazier argues that all meat is not only bad for human beings, but also bad for the world food supply. Do you agree with his viewpoint? Explain your answer. Does the information in Michael Friscolanti's article add anything to Brazier's argument?

Chapter 4

1. The authors in this chapter argue about the relationship of world trade on food prices. After reading these viewpoints, do you think there is a way of improving the global price of food? Explain your answer.

Organizations to Contact

The editors have compiled the following list of organizations concerned with the issues debated in this book. The descriptions are derived from materials provided by the organizations. All have publications or information available for interested readers. The list was compiled on the date of publication of the present volume; the information provided here may change. Be aware that many organizations take several weeks or longer to respond to inquiries, so allow as much time as possible.

Alliance for Global Food Security

50 F Street NW, Suite 900, Washington, DC   20001
(202) 879-0835 • fax: (202) 626-8899
e-mail: elevinson@elevinson.com
Web site: www.globalfoodsecurity.info

The mission of the Alliance for Global Food Security is to address hunger, malnutrition, and food insecurity through the effective and accountable use of funds, food aid, and other resources. The alliance works to assure that food security policies including food aid, emergency response, agriculture development, and nutrition address the realities that alliance members experience firsthand. The alliance's Web site offers a wealth of resources for visitors, including stories from the field and news articles about global food security issues.

European Commission: Directorate-General for Health and Consumers

Health and Consumers Directorate-General, B-1049
Brussels, Belgium
Web site: http://ec.europa.eu/dgs/health_consumer/mailbox/index_en.htm

The Directorate-General for Health and Consumers ensures food and consumer goods sold in the European Union (EU) are safe, that the EU's internal market works for the benefit of consumers, and that Europe helps protect and improve its citizens' health. In order to succeed in its mission, the organization works with other EU institutions, national governments and agencies, consumer organizations, health interest groups, business groups, scientists, researchers, and experts. The Web site offers access to a number of fact sheets from baby food safety to food poisoning.

Food and Agriculture Organization of the United Nations (FAO)

Viale delle Terme di Caracalla, Rome   00153
  Italy
(+39) 06 57051 • fax: (+39) 06 570 53152
e-mail: FAO-HQ@fao.org
Web site: www.fao.org

The Food and Agriculture Organization (FAO) is a United Nations subgroup that leads international efforts to defeat hunger. Serving both developed and developing countries, FAO acts as a neutral forum where all nations meet as equals to negotiate agreements and debate policy. In addition to fact sheets on world hunger, the FAO has available on its Web site annual reports and publications, including *The State of Food Insecurity in the World*.

Food Standards Australia New Zealand

55 Blackall Street, BARTON ACT 2600
  Australia
(+61) 2 6271 2222 • fax: (+61) 2 6271 2278
Web site: www.foodstandards.gov.au

Food Standards Australia New Zealand is a binational government agency. Its main responsibility is to develop and administer the Australia New Zealand Food Standards Code (the Code), which lists requirements for foods relating to additives, food safety, labeling, and genetically modified organisms. The organization's Web site offers tip sheets for citizens, such as "Nutrition Advice for Pregnant Women," and more in-depth reports, including *Bisphenol A (BPA) and Food Packaging*.

Ghana Ministry of Food and Agriculture (MOFA)

PO Box M37, Accra
  Ghana
021-662961
e-mail: info@mofa.gov.gh
Web site: www.ghanaweb.com

The main goal of the Ghana Ministry of Food and Agriculture (MOFA) is to create an environment for sustainable growth and development in the agricultural sector that would include food security, supply of raw materials for industry, and the reduction in poverty and the creation of wealth. Other goals include support for environmental sustainability and cultural values associated with farming. In addition to fact sheets, MOFA publishes reports on its Web site, including *Women in Agriculture*.

Health Canada: Health Products and Food Branch (HPFB)

Brooke Claxton Building, Tunney's Pasture
Ottawa, Ontario   K1A 0K9
  Canada
Web site: www.hc-sc.gc.ca/

The Health Products and Food Branch (HPFB) of Health Canada aims to take an integrated approach to managing the health-related risks and benefits of health products and food. The HPFB's main goals are to minimize health risk factors for Canadians while maximizing the safety provided by the regulatory system for health products and food and to promote conditions that enable Canadians to make healthy choices. In addition to food advisories and other health warnings, the HPFB's Web site includes a number of resources for consumers, such as the section "It's Your Health."

International Association for Food Protection (IAFP)

6200 Aurora Avenue, Suite 200W
Des Moines, IA   50322-2864
(515) 276-3344 • fax: (515) 276-8655

e-mail: info@foodprotection.org
Web site: www.foodprotection.org

The International Association for Food Protection (IAFP) represents a broad range of members with a singular focus—protecting the global food supply. Working together, IAFP members, representing more than fifty countries, help the association achieve its mission through networking, educational programs, journals, career opportunities, and numerous other resources. In addition to fact sheets, the IAFP's Web site provides access to several publications, including the *Journal of Food Protection* and *Food Protection Trends*.

Pan American Health Organization (PAHO)

525 Twenty-third Street NW, Washington, DC   20037
(202) 974-3000 • fax: (202) 974-3663
Web site: http://new.paho.org

The Pan American Health Organization (PAHO) is an international public health agency with more than one hundred years of experience in working to improve health and living standards of the countries of the Americas. It serves as the specialized organization for health of the Inter-American Human Rights System, the Regional Office for the Americas of the World Health Organization, and is part of the United Nations. The PAHO's Web site offers many resources to visitors, including annual reports and the *Pan American Journal of Public Health*.

U.S. Food and Drug Administration (FDA)

10903 New Hampshire Avenue
Silver Spring, MD   20993-0002
1-888-463-6332
Web site: www.fda.gov

The Food and Drug Administration (FDA) is an agency within the U.S. Department of Health and Human Services that regulates food, drugs, tobacco, and other products and services that could potentially harm the American public. The FDA's

Center for Food Safety and Applied Nutrition (CFSAN) works to ensure that the food supply is safe, sanitary, wholesome, and honestly labeled. CFSAN's portion of the FDA's Web site contains a number of resources, including reports on the quality of the food supply and information about how to read food labels.

World Health Organization (WHO)

Avenue Appia 20, Geneva 27   1211
  Switzerland
+41 22 791 21 11 • fax: + 41 22 791 31 11
e-mail: info@who.int
Web site: www.who.int

The World Health Organization (WHO) is the directing and coordinating authority for health within the United Nations system. Foodborne diseases and threats to food safety constitute a growing public health problem, and one of WHO's main missions is to assist its member states to strengthen their programs for improving the safety of food from production to final consumption. WHO's Web site includes a number of excellent resources, including *WHO Global Strategy for Food Safety* and "Ten Facts on Food Safety."

World Trade Organization (WTO)

Rue de Lausanne 154, Geneva 21   CH-1211
  Switzerland
+41 22 739 51 11 • fax: + 41 22 731 42 06
e-mail: enquiries@wto.org
Web site: www.wto.org

The World Trade Organization (WTO) is the only international organization dealing with the global rules of trade between nations. Its main function is to ensure that trade flows as smoothly, predictably, and freely as possible. In addition to statistics about food organizations, the WTO also publishes reports about food safety and security, including *The Global Food Crisis: What Is the Role of Trade?* and *Trade Liberalization and the Right to Food.*

Bibliography of Books

The following books have been selected to supplement the diverse views presented in this book.

Gustavo V. Barbosa-Cánovas et al., eds.
Global Issues in Food Science and Technology. Amsterdam: Elsevier/ Academic Press, 2009.

Warren Belasco
Food: The Key Concepts. Oxford: Berg, 2008.

Julia Cooper, Urs Niggli, and Carlo Leifert, eds.
Handbook of Organic Food Safety and Quality. Cambridge, UK: Woodhead, 2007.

Gavin Fridell
Fair Trade Coffee: The Prospects and Pitfalls of Market-Driven Social Justice. Toronto, ON: University of Toronto Press, 2007.

Nancy Irven
Please Don't Eat the Wallpaper! The Teenager's Guide to Avoiding Trans Fats, Enriched Wheat and High Fructose Corn Syrup. Garden City, NY: Morgan James Pub., 2008.

Richard Lawley, Laurie Curtis, and Judy Davis
The Food Safety Hazard Guidebook. Cambridge, UK: RSC Publishing, 2008.

Howard D. Leathers, Phillips Foster
The World Food Problem: Toward Ending Undernutrition in the Third World. Boulder, CO: Lynne Rienner Publishers, 2009.

Sarah Levete — *Toxins in the Food Chain*. New York: Crabtree Publishing Company, 2010.

Muriel Lightbourne — *Food Security, Biological Diversity, and Intellectual Property Rights*. Burlington, VT: Ashgate, 2009.

William Lockeretz, ed. — *Organic Farming: An International History*. Wallingford, UK: CABI, 2007.

Peter Luetchford — *Fair Trade and a Global Commodity: Coffee in Costa Rica*. London: Pluto Press, 2008.

Terry Marsden et al. — *The New Regulation and Governance of Food: Beyond the Food Crisis?* New York: Routledge, 2010.

Cormac Ó Gráda — *Famine: A Short History*. Princeton, NJ: Princeton University Press, 2009.

Wayne Roberts — *The No-Nonsense Guide to World Food*. Oxford, UK: New Internationalist, 2008.

Ellen Rodger — *Reducing Your Foodprint: Farming, Cooking, and Eating for a Healthy Planet*. St. Catharines, ON: Crabtree Publishing Company, 2010.

Yves Segers, Jan Bieleman, and Erik Buyst, eds. — *Exploring the Food Chain: Food Production and Food Processing in Western Europe, 1850–1990*. Turnhout, Belgium: Brepols Publishers, 2009.

D. John Shaw — *World Food Security: A History Since 1945*. New York: Palgrave Macmillan, 2007

V. Kerry Smith, Carol Mansfield, and Aaron Strong	*Public or Private Production of Food Safety: What Do U.S. Consumers Want?* Cambridge, MA: National Bureau of Economic Research, 2008.
Douglas Southgate, Douglas H. Graham, and Luther Tweeten	*The World Food Economy.* Malden, MA: Blackwell, 2006.
Jeremy Stranks	*The A-Z of Food Safety.* London: Thorogood Publishing, 2007.
Alex von Holy and Denise Lindsay, eds.	*Food Safety: Thinking Globally Acting Locally.* Bradford, England: Emerald Group Publishing, 2006.
Ellen Wall, Barry Smit, and Johanna Wandel, eds.	*Farming in a Changing Climate: Agricultural Adaptation in Canada.* Vancouver, BC: University of British Columbia Press, 2007.
Paul Weirich, ed.	*Labeling Genetically Modified Food: The Philosophical and Legal Debate.* Oxford, UK: Oxford University Press, 2008.
Robin Wheeler	*Food Security for the Faint of Heart: Keeping Your Larder Full in Lean Times.* Gabriola Island, BC: New Society Publishers, 2008.

Index

Geographic headings and page numbers in **boldface** refer to viewpoints about that country or region.